Genta Gusho

Economics & Material Platform of Bidirectional Transceiver for POF

Genta Gusho

Economics & Material Platform of Bidirectional Transceiver for POF

Plastic Optical Fiber

LAP LAMBERT Academic Publishing

Impressum / Imprint

Bibliografische Information der Deutschen Nationalbibliothek: Die Deutsche Nationalbibliothek verzeichnet diese Publikation in der Deutschen Nationalbibliografie; detaillierte bibliografische Daten sind im Internet über http://dnb.d-nb.de abrufbar.
Alle in diesem Buch genannten Marken und Produktnamen unterliegen warenzeichen-, marken- oder patentrechtlichem Schutz bzw. sind Warenzeichen oder eingetragene Warenzeichen der jeweiligen Inhaber. Die Wiedergabe von Marken, Produktnamen, Gebrauchsnamen, Handelsnamen, Warenbezeichnungen u.s.w. in diesem Werk berechtigt auch ohne besondere Kennzeichnung nicht zu der Annahme, dass solche Namen im Sinne der Warenzeichen- und Markenschutzgesetzgebung als frei zu betrachten wären und daher von jedermann benutzt werden dürften.

Bibliographic information published by the Deutsche Nationalbibliothek: The Deutsche Nationalbibliothek lists this publication in the Deutsche Nationalbibliografie; detailed bibliographic data are available in the Internet at http://dnb.d-nb.de.
Any brand names and product names mentioned in this book are subject to trademark, brand or patent protection and are trademarks or registered trademarks of their respective holders. The use of brand names, product names, common names, trade names, product descriptions etc. even without a particular marking in this works is in no way to be construed to mean that such names may be regarded as unrestricted in respect of trademark and brand protection legislation and could thus be used by anyone.

Coverbild / Cover image: www.ingimage.com

Verlag / Publisher:
LAP LAMBERT Academic Publishing
ist ein Imprint der / is a trademark of
OmniScriptum GmbH & Co. KG
Heinrich-Böcking-Str. 6-8, 66121 Saarbrücken, Deutschland / Germany
Email: info@lap-publishing.com

Herstellung: siehe letzte Seite /
Printed at: see last page
ISBN: 978-3-659-53457-7

Zugl. / Approved by: Boston MA , MIT, 2005

Understanding the Economics and Material Platform of Bidirectional Transceiver for
Plastic Optical Fiber

by

Genta (Meco) Gusho

BA Physics
University of Tirana, 1994

SUBMITTED TO THE DEPARTMENT OF MATERIALS SCIENCE AND
ENGINERRING IN PARTIAL FULFILLMENT OF THE REQUIREMENTS FOR THE
DEGREE OF

MASTER OF ENGINEERING IN MATERIALS SCIENCE
AT THE
MASSACHUSETTS INSTITUTE OF TECHNOLOGY

September 2005

© 2005 Genta Gusho. All Rights Reserved.

Signature of Author:_____
Department of Materials Science and Engineering
August 2, 2005,

Certified by:_____
Lionel C. Kimerling
Thomas Lord Professor of Materials Science and Engineering
Thesis Supervisor

Certified by:_____
Randolph E Kirchain Jr,
Assistant Professor of Material Science and Engineering & Engineering Systems
Thesis Supervisor

Accepted by:_____
Gerbrand Ceder
R.P. Simmons Professor of Materials Science and Engineering Chair,
Departmental Committee on Graduate Students

Understanding the Economics and the Material Platform of Bidirectional Transceiver for
Plastic Optical Fiber

by

Genta (Meco) Gusho

Submitted to the Department of Materials Science and Engineering on August 5, 2005 in
partial fulfillment of the requirements for the Degree of Master of Engineering in
Material Science

Abstract

        Limitations of electrical wires result in distortion and dispersion of the signal for
long distances. That have emerged optical communication as the only way of
communication for long distances. For medium distances optics can support the high data
rates required by the latest applications. Optical networks are becoming the dominant
transmission medium as the data rate required by different applications increases.
The bottleneck for implementing optical instead of electric networks for medium
distances, like local area network, is the cost of the optical components and the cost of
replacing the existing copper network. This thesis will discuss the possible cost benefits
that come from the use of different materials like plastic optical fiber instead of silica
fiber or Si, Si/Ge instead of InP or GaAs for the transceiver as well as the trade offs
between the performance and cost when discrete transceiver is replaced by the
monolithically integrated transceiver, by using a process based cost model.

Thesis Supervisor: Lionel C. Kimerling
Title: Thomas Lord Professor of Materials Science and Engineering
Randolph E Kirchain Jr,
Title: Assistant Professor of Material Science and Engineering & Engineering System Division

Acknowledgements.

There are a lot of people who have made it possible for me to be at this stage, and have helped me in my academic and personal growth. I would like to thank sincerely all of them.
First, thanks to Prof. Kimerling for his constant guidance. During the course of my research he has always been very encouraging. I have learned a lot of from him,.
I would like to thank Prof.Kirchain for getting me interested in the area of cost analysis. He has been providing valuable advice and guidance whenever required. I would also like to thank him for reading my thesis and giving me excellent critiques.
EMAT Students has been very helpful with their discussions and their advise.
My sister, Irma and my friend Abe reminded me at regular intervals of possible life after M.Eng.
I would like to thank especially my husband Lajdi and my daughter Zheni for motivating me to finish my thesis and making it a worthwhile experience. Thanks to them, this year has been easier for me and filled with laughs.
Finally, I would like to thank my parents who have always given me their unconditional support and without whom I would never have made it here in the first place.

Table of Contents

Chapter 1
Introduction

Due to the capacity limitations of electrical wires (distortion from dispersion and interference result in a signal that can not be read if transmitted at high frequencies), all long distance communication is done through optics. For medium distance communication, e.g. local area networks, optics is making significant progress because only optics can support the high data rates required by the latest applications. At shorter distances (a few meters - few hundred meters), primarily in data links, optics is rapidly introduced. Researchers are working to use optics for communication purposes even at short scales such as board-to-board, chip-to-chip, and on-chip [1].Optical is becoming the dominant transmission medium as the data rate required by different applications increases.

The requirements for components of optical networks vary with the optical networks in which they are deployed. Especially the distances have direct consequences on the types of performance needed. In long haul and long haul networks, component performance is critical and cost is secondary. The requirement for low loss components is critical because amplification is expensive and it should be minimized. In metro core networks, performance and cost are important. Since the distances for residential networks are relatively short, the loss and dispersion requirements are lower compare to long distances requirements. Cost reduction of the optical system components becomes more important for short distance networks.

This thesis will assess the trade offs between the performance and cost for the transceiver and the fiber for short distances. With the increase of the demand for more bandwidth and cheaper components, plastic optical fiber (POF) has emerged as the most feasible choice for local area network (LAN) applications. Market researchers [2] project growth in available market for POF in various fields as given in table 1.

YEAR	Premise wiring	Inter-connections	Consumer	Industrial	Auto	Medical	TOTAL (US $)
2003	20	46	157	150	187	55	615
2004	26	54	193	176	262	64	775
2005	43	73	228	212	335	73	964
2006	67	81	269	233	394	84	1,128
2007	89	102	300	278	473	94	1,336
2008	117	124	374	328	567	105	1,615

Source: Beach Communications

Table 1 Available market for POF in various fields 2003-2008, $Millions [3]

Beside the transmission medium, optical transceiver is the other key component in optical network because it is the interface between electrical and optical signal. Very sophisticated optics and components are available for long distance communication through silica fibers, however new technology is needed for POF because the requirements are very different for short distances. The driving force in developing a new transceiver is again the demand that have emerged for low cost optical components. The low cost transceiver that could be cheaply installed into personal electronics, automobiles, or other applications promise to help optoelectronic industry reach economies of scale.

This thesis seeks to address the current state of the optical transceiver, plastic optical fiber and the market for their LAN applications. In this thesis the issues involved in designing POF transceiver, POF itself and the impact of those choices in the cost of the product are examined using a process based cost modeling. We will start with Section 1.1 explaining the need for high capacity and high speed networks. Then Section 1.2 will introduce the benefits of using POF on optical system communication and also the technology of transceiver will be briefly explained; Section 1.3 will introduce the process based cost modeling (PBCM). Finally, Section 1.4 will be giving an overview of all the chapters.

1.1 The Need for High Speed in LAN

Digital transmission systems with a high bit rate were before exclusively used in telecommunications for long range transmissions. The field of local computer networks was dominated by copper wires that completely satisfied the typical data rates of up to 10 Mbitps [4], when there was hardly any demand for high data rates. During the nineties, after data communication for long haul transmission had become completely digitalized the development of digital systems for private users started on a massive scale. Digital end user equipment has been introduced everywhere, CD, DVD (digital video disk), digital TV, PC and digital telephone connections (ISDN), video conferencing , remote library service, video interacting, classes on line. With offers such as T-DSL (ADSL technology provided by Deutsche Telekom AG) as well as fast internet access via satellite or broadband digital services on the broadband cable network, private users are being offered access to additional applications that didn't exist before. Increase of Internet traffic has result in an increasing need for high bandwidth network components .Figure 1 shows the growth in information carrying capacity of the transmission medium.

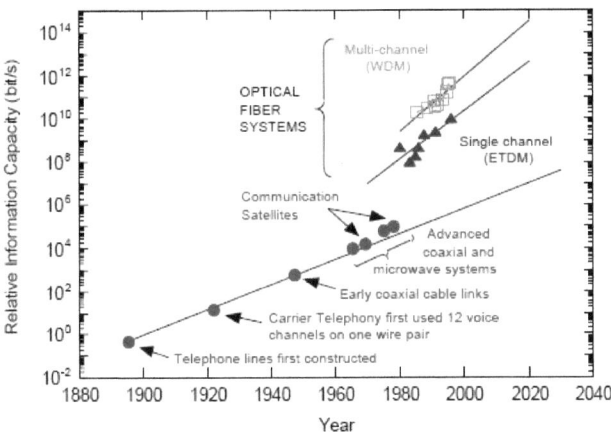

Figure 1 Growth in information carrying capacity of a single communications line over time (© Kimerling 2003)

Network components are standardized. Ethernet is the most popular network. The Ethernet protocol is used on 80 % to 85 % of the world's LAN connected PC's and work stations because it has been adapted to meet the needs of customers at low prices [5] Ethernet networks have been defined by the IEEE 802 standardization committee [6] ,

10-megabit Ethernet was standardized in 1988, Gigabit Ethernet in 1998 and 10-gigabit Ethernet, is currently close to approval (for more the reader is referred to http://standards.ieee.org/getieee802 . The 10 Gigabit Ethernet standard is the first Ethernet standard with a physical layer definition for both LAN and WAN. While the electrical implementation of gigabit Ethernet over twisted pairs is limited in distance to 100 m, the optical solutions based on 850 nm, 1300nm and 1500 nm, in reality cover distances up to respectively 1 km, 10 km and 70 km [7]. Table 2 gives and overview of the maximal transmission distance for different physical media, as defined in the Gigabit Ethernet standard.

Type of fibre	wavelength	Distance	
		Gigabit Ethernet standard	In reality
Multimode fibre, 50um core	850nm	550m	1km
Multimode fibre, 62.5um core	850nm	275m	
Multimode fibre	1310nm	2km	

Table 2 The maximal transmission distance for different physical media, as defined in the Gigabit Ethernet standard [7]

Gigabit Ethernet will be a standard physical layer in office LAN and home networks. The steadily growth of traffic volumes into WAN and LAN therefore offers new markets for optical components. Smaller, faster, more complex and less expensive component solutions are needed. .RHK's market forecast [8] for global entertainment is given in figure 2.

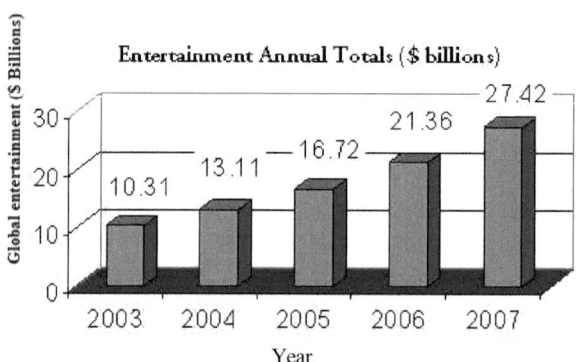

Figure 2 RHK's forecast for entertainment annual growth rates 2002-2007 [8]

All the examples given above and the forecast for the high bandwidth increasing demand demonstrate that completely new markets for digital transmission systems are being developed for short range applications. Investment dollars are shifting from the core to metro networks.

1.2 POF in optical system communication and the technology of the optical transceiver.

1.2.1 Advantages of POF system communication

The optical fiber communication is established as the main communication system because the requirements for more bandwidth are over passing the copper capacity. Optical fiber offers low loss over a high bandwidth, low levels of undesirable transmission impairments, immunity to electromagnetic interference, and long life-spans compare to Cu-based systems (more about limitations of Cu on Chapter 2). Besides the optical fiber communication the other alternative for optical network is wireless communications. We can think of optical fiber and wireless communications as quite complementary. Wireless goes almost everywhere, but provides a highly bandwidth-constrained transmission channel, susceptible to a variety of impairments [9]. Optical fiber, on the other hand, doesn't go everywhere, but where it does go, it provides a huge amount of available bandwidth.

Optical fiber can be silica or plastic fiber. Even though the perfection in performance of silica fibers is not achievable (to date) from plastic ones, the main disadvantages of the silica fiber such as connector cost, skilled labor, fragility-microfractures/microbends and the steadily growth demand for cheaper LAN components, have offered interesting opportunities for plastic optical fiber. POF compete with copper wires, coaxial cables, glass optical fibers, and wireless.

The plastic optical fiber originally developed by DuPont in 1968 had a step index profile, and this technology is the most mature [10]. Manufacturers form POFs out of plastic materials such as polystyrene, polycarbonates, and polymethyl methacrylate (PMMA). Due to incomplete purification of the source materials used, attenuation was in the beginning in the range of 1000dB/km.

During the seventies it became possible to reduce losses near to 125dB/km at 650nm wavelength. The high loss problem is being addressed constantly and researchers have brought losses down to potentially 10 dB/km [12] .

In 1997, Asahi Glass Co. [11] successfully developed a perfluorinated (PF) GI POF, which has less than one-third of attenuation of conventional PMMA. Figure 3 shows the attenuation spectrum of PF GI-POF.

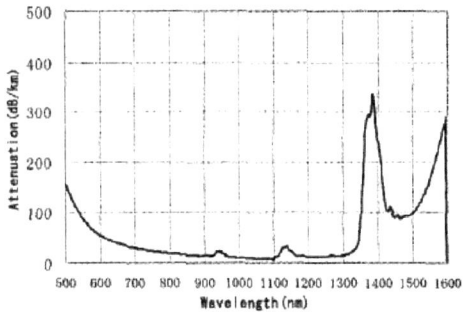

Figure 3 Attenuation spectrum of PF GI-POF [11]

Gigabit Ethernet transmission experiments using PF GI-POF over record distances in the order of 1 km and at wavelengths in the 850 and 1300 nm area are reported [13]. Polymer optical fibers are cheaper than silica fibers and can meet many of the requirements for digital transmission systems that are developing for short range application. Therefore they have become the choice for short range optical networks today.

1.2.2 The technology of transceiver

So, what is an optical system consist of beside the optical fiber (or the transmission medium) ? It has the transmitter and the receiver. In digital circuits, binary data in the form of voltage are transmitted. Data in the form of these voltage levels is fed to a transmitter driver, which converts these levels into the voltage or current signal required to drive the optical transmitter device. The optical transmitter device converts these electrical signals into the modulation of light beams, which then travel through some propagation medium to the destination. The photodiode on the receiver side converts the optical signal into current, which is then converted into logic level by the receiver. One example of the transceiver chip is given in figure 4.

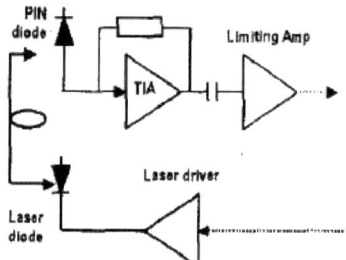

Figure 4 Transmitter and the receiver chip [14]

A receiver consists of a photodiode, TIA and limiting amplifier consisting of electrical circuits. Transmission devices can be LED, laser or VCSEL. VCSEL are strong candidate as transmitter devices (more on this on Chapter 4). Various optical transmitter technologies are explained and compared in literature [15], [16] . From different light sources that can be used for POF transceiver, VCSEL operating at 850nm actually represent the majority of commercialization [17] With the increasing demand for data communications through cheaper optical networks, the cost effective POF transceivers have become increasingly of interest.

1.3 Introduction to process based cost modeling

The following section explains how Process Base Cost Modeling (PBCM) works and the results for the cost of the product incorporating yield of integrated and discrete transceiver; for more understanding on PBCM the reader is refer to [18], [19], [20],[21].

Process-Based Cost Modeling

Cost models have been developed to avoid expensive strategic errors in product development and deployment. Models allow the exploration of key decision parameters through analytical methods rather than through time-consuming and potentially expensive experimentation and prototyping. Ideally, this capability allows decision makers to understand the physical consequences of their technical choices before those choices are put into action [19]. In this thesis process based cost modeling is used to project the manufacturing cost of different transceiver. Design options studied are :1) discrete photodiodes and TIA using ball lens in one case, 2) discrete photodiodes and TIA not using a ball lens but molding half sphere lens on transparent resin3) integrated photodiode and TIA on Si .

The cost of the transceiver is a function of both the processes used and the design chosen for the specific product. Some of the varied costs that are taken into consideration in the model are: Material, Energy, Labor, Primary Equipment, Auxiliary Equipment, Warehousing, Installation Expense, Maintenance Expense, Tools, Molds, Dies, Building Space, Skilled labor, unskilled labor, and Overhead Labor. Based on process flow (given on Appendix A) for the specific transceiver operating conditions that describe the process are projected in the model. To make a successful cost forecast in the spreadsheet model, it is necessary to identify the type and the order of processes required to produce the device. When defining the process flow necessary to produce a device, process type and order must by augmented by a description of the materials, actions, and operating conditions occurring at a given process step [17]. In the model, the specific recipe for the model to use at that process step is entered with the set of inputs describing the resource materials consumption.
Example: Process- Plasma etch
Incidental Yield
Embedded yield
Machine Cost
Capital Dedication(Y/N)
Capital Usage life
Max. Batch Size
Average Batch Size
Direct Labor: Higher Ed.
Direct Labor: Technician
Direct Labor: Skilled.
Direct Labor: Unskilled
Installation Cost (%)

Maintenance Cost (%)
Auxiliary Equipment (%)
Operating Time per Batch
Setup time per Batch
Maintenance Freq.
Tool/Mask Initial investment
Tool/Mask Additional Unit Cost
High-Grade Cleanroom Space

   The focus of the cost analysis would be on the implication of integration on cost for the different transceivers design considered. Three possible designs are analyzed in cost model- 1.Discrete components and discrete package, 2. Discrete components, only receiver packaged separately, 3. Monolithically integrated device. For each of the different transceivers dominant costs areas and the improvements that offer the best opportunities to lower cost are identify.

1.4 Overview of the remaining chapters.

The limitation of electric wiring, different POF index of refraction profile, in general terms and using examples, and also POF materials be discussed in chapter 2 . In chapter 3 applications of POF and POF's transceiver will be discussed. Also the market for POF networks will be explored on last section. Chapter 4 gives an overview of the optical receiver technology including basic elements of an optical fiber communication system - the fiber, transmitter (light –emitting diode (LED), laser (edge or vertical surface emitting), and the receiver (positive-intrinsic-negative (PIN) diode, avalanche photodetector (APD) detectors. In chapter 5 discussion about the properties , of silicon that affect the cost and the speed of the device as well as the explanation about the cost benefits that Si offers for the transceiver and also report the level of integration to date, takes place. Chapter 6 will analyze the impact of line dedication to the cost of differently designed optical transceiver, sensitivity of unit cost to annual production volume, results from the technology change on the cost using process based cost model and the identification of cost drivers for individual processes. Lastly, the conclusions drawn from the thesis will be presented.

Chapter 2 Plastic Optical Fiber for Communication Systems

This chapter will discuss the limitation of electric wiring, different POF index of refraction profile, in general terms and using examples, and also POF materials.

2.1 The limitation of electric wiring

The benefits of optical systems compare to Cu-based systems are well-known, however to date broadband is currently mostly provided over traditional phone lines (DSL), cable networks (cable modem service), and in some cases wireless networks. Recommendations for Ethernet for the First Mile (EFM) [22] . to use "Ethernet-over-xDSL Adaptation Layer"that fits on the γ-interface, existing G.99x as physical layers for EFM, covering all the rate/reach objectives, have been done. Regarding the replacement of the copper twisted pair, the case has been: Nothing beats reusing existing things when it comes to "time to market". Fiber-optic infrastructures are technologically attractive for fixed access networks as well as mobile networks but represent significant investments. It is shown [23] that today, fiber-optic solutions are, in general, more expensive than both twisted copper pair and microwave radio solutions. However, the optimum infrastructure depends on the specific network scenario. The techno-economic analysis of mobile network infrastructures analyze fiber-optic star, tree, and ring infrastructures compared to twisted copper pair star and microwave radio tree infrastructures. (Data link configurations include rings-each receiver on a network responds only to its address, stars -signals go to a hub for relay, and ring-all receivers are interconnected in a manner similar to the Internet). The analysis [23] shows that, different infrastructures are favorable for different types of networks. For example twisted copper pair star infrastructures are favorable for small to medium sized networks with small cells (10–500 m), but future upgrade possibilities are limited. In most cases, fiber-optic infrastructures have the highest installation costs. These costs cover a large number of factors such as maintenance, repair, power consumption, supervision, etc. The advantages (at the moment) of the twisted cooper pair infrastructure do not necessarily translate into the cheapest infrastructure installation after five or ten years. The fiber-optic is the only infrastructures that offers cable and equipment failure protection and have the best possibilities for future upgrades.

It is important to understand the limitations and issues Cu-based systems to realize the need of optical systems. Immune to cross talk is an advantage of optical systems. Optical communication is accomplished by sending photons between two physically separate transmitting and receiving nodes. Especially for the applications of optics on interconnects to silicon chips (explained in more details [1]) this property of optics is quite useful. The voltages on the two sides need not be related to each other and can be completely electrically isolated. This provides noise immunity from one side to the other. With scaling in electronic chips, supply currents are increasing and so are resistive drops in DC supply and ground bounce effects. Hence this voltage isolation property of optics may become progressively more important for future generations. Loss is very significant in electrical wires at high frequencies because of the skin effect.

Ethernet over twisted pairs is limited in distance to 100 m. One of the main advantages of optical fiber compare to Cu wire is the higher capacity in caring data. Figure 5 shows that the capacity of a bundle of Cu wires can be replaced by one single optic fiber.

Figure 5 The capacity of each of those bundles of Cu wires can be replaced by one single optic fiber.

Advantages offered by fiber-optic interconnects relative to metallic interconnects, include the twenty times greater bandwidth x distance product, ten times lower interchannel skew, and ten times density improvement.
Summary of the advantages and disadvantages of Cu wires or optical fiber is represented on table 3

Choice	Advantages	Disadvantages
Twisted pair wire	low installation cost	low bandwidth, susceptible to noise ,speed =56kbps
Coaxial Cable	Ground is shielded (immune to interference)	amplifiers every mile , cable easily tapped =low security, speed= 2.5 Mbps(for Cu marine cables)
Fiber optic Cable	Immune to cross talk, high security, high bandwidth capacity over Cu wire, faster transmission, possibilities of transmitting data , video, graphics, environment friendly(emit no radiation), doesn't rust, light weight, Faster transmission-400 times rate of copper wires	Connector cost, skilled labor, fragility- microfractures/microbends,

Table 3 advantages and disadvantages of twisted pair wire, coaxial cable, fiber optic

In conclusion, to date practicable and proven solutions do exist for copper cables, too. One example of such solution would be the way data networks in office buildings, is set up in Germany. In contrast to U.S.A. shielded cables dominate in Germany. Consequently, electromagnetic disturbance is not a disadvantage for copper wires when properly installed. However optical fibers offer more speed and bandwidth for LAN applications. Applications like the digitalization of diverse entertainment media (music, video, TV) are requiring more and more bandwidth and speed that copper so far has offered; this would leave optical fiber the only choice for communication medium.

2.2 POF

The idea of guiding light is first patent by Daniel Colladon, 1841. He first demonstrated that light can be guided within a water jet. Figure 6 is taken from his patent ,Pat.# 247229.

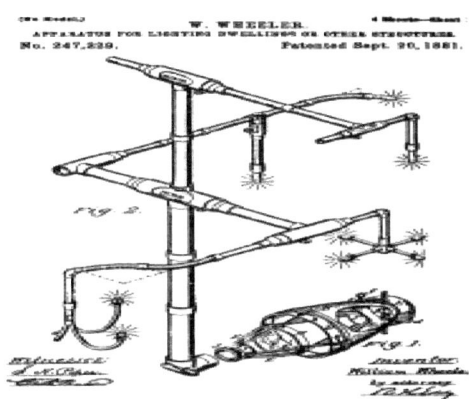

Figure 6 Guiding light through water jet [24]

Since then the idea of guiding light has evolved and today light can be guided through optical fibers using the total internal reflection given by Snell's law as shown in figure 7.

Snell's law

$$\frac{\sin \theta_1}{\sin \theta_2} = \frac{n_2}{n_1}$$

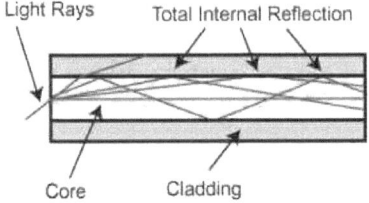

Figure 7 Total internal reflection

The light is guided down the centre of the fiber called the "core". The core is surrounded by an optical material called the "cladding" that traps the light in the core using total internal reflection. Fiber is coated with a protective plastic covering called the "primary buffer coating" that protects it from moisture and other damage. More protection is provided by the outer covering called a "jacket".

The signal (short pulses of light) disperses when it travels through the length of the fiber, as shown in figure 8.

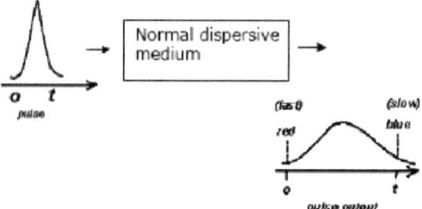

Figure 8 Broadening of the pulse due to dispersive medium [25]

Dispersion refers initially to all processes that result in a difference in the transit time of various modes. One mode is a propagation condition of the light that is uniquely defined by the wavelength, polarization and propagation path. Dispersion can be mode dispersion and chromatic dispersion. Mode dispersion is due to the fact that light paths have different lengths in multimode fiber. To get around this problem design choices can be chosen as explained in section 2.2.1. Chromatic dispersion exists because of the influence of the spectral width of a transmitter on a temporal broadening of the input pulse. The way to minimize this type of dispersion, as explained in 2.2.2 is to minimize the material dispersion and waveguide dispersion.

The figure of merit (FOM) for the fiber would be as given in equation (1),

$$FOM = Distance \,/(t_{response} * D_\lambda) \qquad (1)$$

where : Distance is given in km and shows the length of the fiber, $t_{response}$ is the response time in seconds, D_λ is the dispersion coefficient that measures the temporal spread/length*spectral width

2.2.1 Singlemode & Multimode fibers

Singlemode fiber has a smaller core, so that the light travels in only one ray. Singlemode Fiber shrinks the core down so small that the light can only travel in one ray. This increases the bandwidth to almost infinity - but it's practically limited to about 100,000 gigahertz. Usually it is used when dealt with long haul telecom or submarine cables.

Multimode fiber has light traveling in the core in many rays, called modes. It has a bigger core then single mode fiber and is used with LED sources at wavelengths of 850 and 1300 nm for slower local area networks (LANs) and lasers at 850 and 1310 nm for networks running at gigabits per second or more.

Step index multimode was the first Fiber design but is too slow for most uses, due to the dispersion caused by the different path lengths of the various modes. Step index fiber is rare in design today. Graded index multimode fiber uses variations in the composition of the core to compensate for the different path lengths of the modes. It offers hundreds of times more bandwidth than step index fiber. Figure 8 shows light guidance within the single mode and multi mode fiber

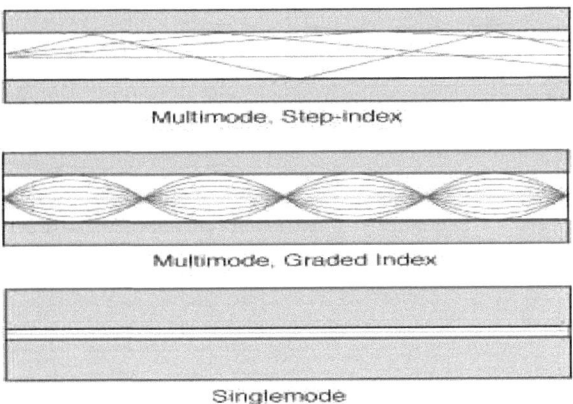

Multimode, Step-index

Multimode, Graded Index

Singlemode

Figure 8 Light guidance within multi mode step-index, multi mode graded index and single mode fiber

Another way to engineer the refractive index profile, is given in figure 9 [26]

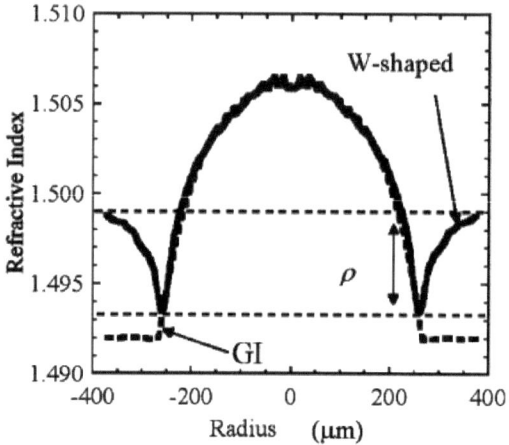

Figure 9 Measured refractive index profile of the W-shaped and GI POFs. Solid line: W-shaped POF.
Broken line: GI POF.[26]

The W-shaped POF is used to increase the bandwidth through model dispersion compensation. Each mode propagates having its own group delay, which means a small mode coupling in the W-shaped POF as well. The group delay difference between the highest and lowest order modes is much smaller than that in the GI POF. This delay time contraction is caused not by the mode coupling but by the modal dispersion compensation effect of the refractive index valley. W-shaped POF has a valley of the refractive index at the boundary of the core and cladding of the conventional GI POF. W-shaped index of refraction profile influences the group delay of higher order modes more and therefore gives better compensation for the modal dispersion that GI POF

2.2.2 Materials used for POF

When people mention optical fiber, most of them think of silica fibers even though plastic fibers are fabricated as early as the silica fibers. The reason is that because of high losses the plastic fiber could not keep up with silica fiber. Said this is clear that, the reduction of optical loss of POFs is a major challenge for materials scientists. The factors that contribute in optical loss for POF are intrinsic and extrinsic. In the intrinsic factors absorption (higher harmonics of C-H absorption and electronic transitions), and Rayleigh scattering (refractive index fluctuations, orientation & composite fluctuations) are included. Extrinsic losses are because of absorption (transition metals, absorbed water) and from scattering (dust, fractures, core- cladding boundary imperfections ect.).

Polymer materials exhibit strong absorption due the exciting molecular vibrations of their bonds like C-H, C-F, or C-O. The position of the fundamental vibration absorption of molecular bonds is in table 4

Molecular group	Vibration absorption [μm]
C–H	3.3 – 3.5
C–D	4.4
C–F	8.0
C=O	5.3 – 6.5
C–C	7.9 – 10.0
C–O	7.9 – 10.0
C–Cl	11.7 – 18.2
O–H	2.8

Table 4 The position of the fundamental vibration absorption of molecular bonds [27]

The absorption of light due to molecular vibrations in macromolecules is considered by treating individual bonds on a monomeric unit to be as an uncoupled system of anharmonic oscillators. To calculate the loss per bond as a function of wavelength one need to sum over the number of such bonds in each repeat unit and multiplies by the molecular weight to approximate the cumulative contribution of that type of bond. The energy levels associated with uncoupled anharmonic oscillators are determined using a Morse potential [28] of the form

$$M(v) = v_e \left(v + \tfrac{1}{2}\right) - v_o N \left(v + \tfrac{1}{2}\right)^2 \qquad (3)$$

where vo is the frequency of the fundamental vibration given by equation 4

$$v = \frac{1}{2\pi} * \sqrt{k/\mu} \qquad (4)$$

k is the spring constant and μ is the reduced mass of the bond, $v = 0, 1, 2, 3, \ldots$ is the harmonic number, and $\aleph$ is the bond anharmonicity constant. The reader is referred to [29] for more about the calculation of the loss in POF.

Absorption losses of polymers are reduced basically by using materials with less or no C-H. Hydrogen is replaced by a heavier atom from the seventh group like fluorine, chlorine and deuterium [30],[31]; as a result the core becomes heavier and its frequency of vibration lowers. The quantum model states that system will absorb at energy values

$E_m = mh_{\omega}$ (m=1,2,...) where $\omega = \sqrt{\dfrac{k}{m}}$. Because of molecular engineering such as

perfluorination and deuteration of polymers, it has become possible to reduce the attenuation < 50 dB/km at the visible and near infrared region of the spectrum [32], [33] Even though the performance of POF has not achieve silica fibers, GI POF transmission has been able to achieve speed equal to 1.2 Gb/s/km with attenuation of 30dB/km [34], [35]

The following material in this section will describe the polymers that are use most frequently; decreasing loss is the order followed.

Core materials

The materials for POF core can be divided in three groups:

- Compounds containing Hydrogen

- Compounds with partial substitution of Hydrogen

- Compounds with complete substitution of Hydrogen

Polymethylmethacrylate

Polymethylmethacrylate (PMMA) or known as Plexiglass is compound containing hydrogen. Molecular structure of PMMA is given in figure 10.

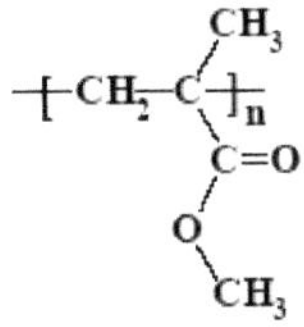

Figure 10 Molecular structure of PMMA

PMMA is building blocks of monomer methyl methacrylate (MMA). MMA is produced from acetone. PMMA is manufactured by free radical polymerization using bulk or suspension technique [36]. Table 4 gives the physical and mechanical constants of PMMA.

Properties	Value	Units	Test procedure
Refractive index	1.491	n_D^{20}	DIN 53491
Density	1.18	g/cm^2	DIN 53479
Tensile strength	80 (72)	MPa	DIN 53455
Charpy impact strength	15	kJ/m^2	ISO 179/1D
Flexural strength	115 (105)	MPa	DIN 53452
Modulus of elasticity	3300	MPa	DIN 53457
Glass transition temperature (T_g)	105	°C	[31]
Co-efficient of thermal expansion		K^{-1}	DIN 53752-A
-Linear	$7*10^{-5}$ (0-50 °C)		
-Volume	$2.72*10^{-4}$ ($< T_g$)		[31]
	$5.80*10^{-4}$ ($> T_g$)		
Shrinkage onset temperature	> 80	°C	[28]
Water absorption	30	mg	DIN 53495

Table 4 Physical and mechanical constants of PMMA [37]

Polystyrene polymer

Polystyrene polymer (PS) have been fabricated first by Toray in 1972, CIS in 1993. PS fibers are supposed to have lower attenuation than PMMA. Attenuation 114dB/km at 670nm are possible for PS [38]

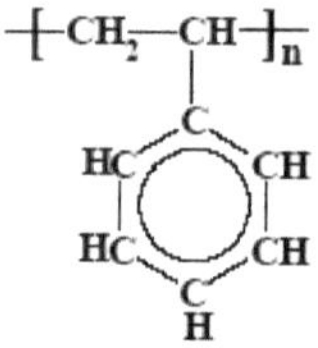

Figure 11 Molecular structure of PS

Deteuterinated polymers

Deteuterinated polymers can be achieved by substituting the hydrogen with heavier atoms. In 1977 Du Pont reported 180dB/km loss at 790nm on the first deuterinated POF; in 1993 Keio University reported 56dB/km loss at 688nm. Having a significant reduction in the absorption losses compare to PMMA make this type of polymer very attractive for low loss applications, but water vapor can be absorbed by the fiber replacing deuterium with hydrogen and bringing the loss go up again.

Fluorinated polymers (FP)

Fluorinated polymers are called polymers that have hydrogen replaced by fluorine. F is many times heavier than H so the absorption band move toward the infra- red. The graded index POF is achieved through doping and co-polymerization. Asahi Glass of Japan together with Keio University has developed a perfluorinated polymer graded index POF with losses less than 25 dB/km over the 850-1300nm range [39] To date transmission rates at distances as given in table 5 have been reported for POF [40]

Year	Bitrate(Gbitps)	Distance (m)	Wavelength(nm)	Organization
1997	2.5	200	1300	Fujitsu
1998	5	200	645	Eindh. Univ.
1998	2.5	300	1310	Eindh. Univ.
1998	2.5	550	840	Lucent
1999	2.5	550	1300	Ulm. Univ.
1999	11	100	950	Eindh. Univ.
1999	7	80	950	Eindh. Univ.
2001	1.25	990	840	Eindh. Univ
2002	1.25	1006	1300	Eindh. Univ.

Table 5 Attenuation reported for fluorinated polymer fibers [40]

Low attenuation FP POF are commercially available see table 6

Product Specifications	
Transmission Characteristics	
Attenuation at 850 nm (dB/km)	≤ 60
Attenuation at 1300 nm (dB/km)	≤ 60
Bandwidth at 850 nm (MHz·km)	≥ 300
Numerical aperture	0.185 ±0.015
Macrobend loss (dB for 10 turns on a 25 mm radius quarter circle)	≤ 0.60
Zero dispersion wavelength (nm)	1200-1650
Dispersion slope (ps/nm²·km)	≤ 0.06
Physical Characteristics	
Core diameter (μm)	120 ±10
Cladding diameter (μm)	490 ±7
Core-cladding concentricity (μm)	≤ 5
Maximum tensile load (N)	7.0
Environmental Performance	
Temperature induced attenuation at 850 nm from −20°C to +70°C (dB/km)	≤ 5
Temperature induced attenuation at 850 nm from +75°C 85% RH 30 day cycle (dB/km)	≤ 10

Table 6 Perfluorinated plastic optical fiber specifications [41]

Gigabit Ethernet Transmission Experiments using GI-POF are reported in [13]. Transmission experiment for GI-POF 1.25 Gbitps at 840 nm is set up as shown in figure 12 and maximum distances of 990m are achieved.

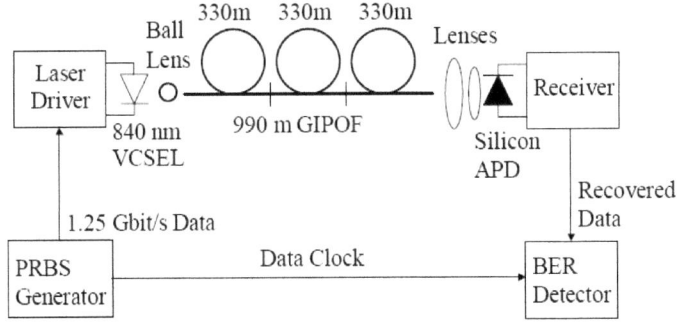

Figure 12   Set up for transmission at 840nm for 990 m distances [13]

Materials of the cladding

The main requirements for cladding materials are: low refractive index (but close to the index of the core material) and good forming ability. The cladding material is mainly composed of a copolymer of long chain fluoroalkyl methacrylate, methyl methacrylate and methacrylic acid. The protective layer material is composed of a copolymer of vinylidenefluoride and tetrafluoroethylene [42] . A variety of cladding polymers, as listed on table 7, have been developed and are commercially available [43].

Monomer	$-R_{F, H}$	T_g [°C]	n_D
Methyl methacrylate	$-CH_3$	105	1.489
2,2,2-trifluoroethyl methacrylate	$-CH_2-CF_3$	69	1.418
2,2,3,3-tetrafluoropropyl methacrylate	$-CH_2-CF_2-CHF_2$	68	1.417– 1.422
2,2,3,3,3-pentafluoropropyl methacrylate	$-CH_2-CF_2-CF_3$	70– 77	1.1395
1,1,1,3,3,3-hexafluoroisopropyl methacrylate	$-CH_2\begin{smallmatrix}CF_3\\ \\CF_3\end{smallmatrix}$	56	1.390
2,2,3,4,4,4-hexafluorobutyl methacrylate	$-CH_2-CHF-CF_2-CF_3$	-	-
2,2,3,3,4,4,4-heptafluorobutyl methacrylate	$-CH_2-CF_2-CF_2-CF_3$	65	1.383

Table 7 Commercially available monomers of poly (fluroalkyl methacrylates) and T_{glass} and n of their homopolymers [43] "R" represents the alkyl group of the monomer methacrylate.

Jacket materials

The jacket should be able to protect the fiber from environment which means should provide thermal resistance, loading or tensile strength, ect. A detailed table with materials for jackets is given in table 8 [44]

Polymer	Allowed operation temperature [°C]	Density [g/cm^{-3}]
Polyvinylchloride (PVC)	70	1.20-1.50
Polyethylene (PE)		
-Low density	70	1.30-1.60
-High density	80	0.95-0.98
Polypropylene	90	0.91
Polyamide 6 (PA 6)	80-90	1.10-1.15
Polyurethane (PU)	90-100	1.15-1.20
Copolymer of Ethylene-Vinylacetate (EVA)	120	1.30-1.50
Perfluoroethylenepropylene (PFEP)	180	2.00-2.30
Polytetrafluoroethylene (PTFE)	260	2.00-2.30

Table 8 Polymers for the use as jacket materials in POFs.[44]

In conclusion, low loss POF have been fabricated and commercialized. The record coupling efficiency between about 80% and 50% [45] and the low loss levels of 25 dB/km at transmission speed 1.25Gbps at distances around 1km, make POF applicable for Gigabit Ethernet applications in customer premises and local area networks.

Chapter 3 Applications of POF, POF transceivers and the market

Plastic optical fibers have many applications in many industries. To date POF has dominated the area like lighting, area that represents only niche markets. The market share of POF in sensor technology and data communications have been small due to better performance offered by silica fibers. However a drastic change has shift in data communication system. The need for Gigabit Ethernet and for lower cost optical component, present a huge demand for POF and POF transceiver. Exciting possibilities exist in optical interconnects at different levels [1] as shown in figure 15.

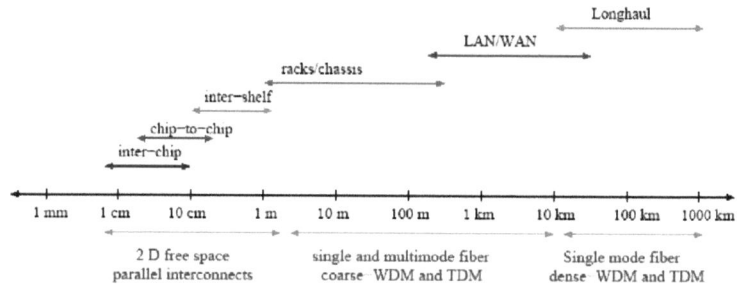

Figure 15 Possibilities of optical interconnects at different levels [1]

World market by application is given in figure 16 . The most significant applications, that bring a boom in the POF & transceiver market, are in :
- Automotive field
- LAN applications

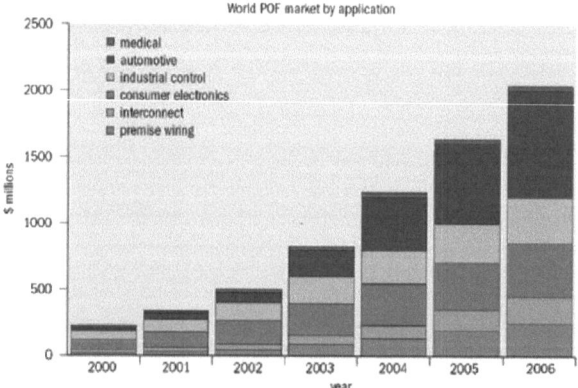

Figure   World market by application [46]

3.1 Applications in the automotive field

German auto manufacturer Daimler-Benz recognized that the increasing use of digital devices in automobiles increased the weight, susceptibility to electro-magnetic interference, and complexity of wiring harnesses so in 1998, polymer optical fiber for the entertainment networks in vehicles was used for the first time. Since POF first use in cars the need for lower cost has brought to creation of standards. Common standards that are developed for car networks with POF to reduce cost are:

- CAN (Controller Area Network)

- D2B (Digital Domestic Bus)

- MOST (Media Oriented System Transport)

- IEEE 1394

- Byteflight

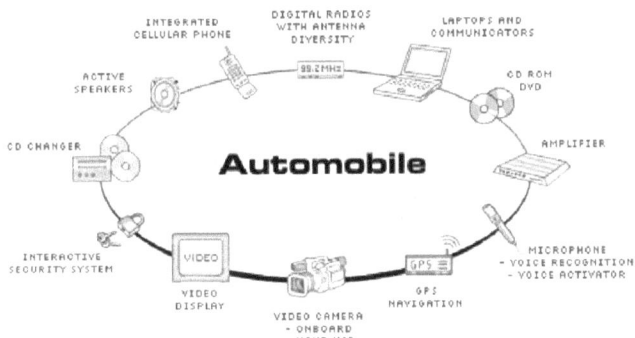

Figure 16 Use of POF in data communication in automobile[47]

At the end of 2003, 19 European models came equipped with POF data buses. Combination of car radios and mobile telephones, traffic guidance, mobile internet, access and DVD player, are offered in today's vehicles. Automobiles have evolved from having electronic media in the vehicle essentially for vehicle control support to having a variety of sophisticated information .Cars today include navigation systems that can work in conjunction with a security system to locate a stolen car. As a result, more capacity and speed is needed from the fiber. The introduction of 50Mbitps and 150Mbps is currently being prepared in the MOST consortium [47] .

3.2 LAN Applications

  To date, copper based network is dominant in LAN. Then, why the demand is going toward POF networks? Applications that require high bandwidth and speed like video-conferencing or classes on line are now available. It will take 2or 3min to download a movie from high-speed network and it will take 6 to 7 hours with electric wires. Even though just a few years ago 10Mbitps Ethernet was the standard, today the increasing demand for speed has set the standard up to 10Gbitps Ethernet. Low cost, capacity and speed offered by POF makes it the choice for LAN. In this section the applications that require high speed and large capacity (resulting in increase of the demand for POF network) are discussed.

TV Anytime

  Development in the television environment has open new possibilities for personal video recorder(PVR). Today's researchers forecast that to future television viewing will be from PVR's rather than real time broadcast sources. The efforts for global interoperability of digital media recording equipment have resulted in three specifications from TV Anytime Forum. TiVo, Replay Networks, WebTV are successfully offering this type of services also called TV Anytime. Customer is attracted to PVC because these devices allow personalization of programming and offer a substantial amount of television programming to be stored on hard disk and played back in non linear fashion.

Interactive Television

  Convergence between television and internet or Interactive television (ITV) represents the goal for future devices. Internet and television are display devices with very profound difference between them. Internet is an interactive (two way) medium carrying static content for point to point distribution and TV is one way medium with dynamic content distributed in point to multipoint fashion. With the proper hardware television programs can be fairly successfully viewed on a personal computer screen. Putting a Web page from the computer to the TV screen is not as straight forward however solutions are provided[48]

Video Conference

  If there is to name a "killer" application for POF and TRx, Video Conference would be it. Due to the high bandwidth requirement and rate variability of compressed video, delivering video across wide area networks is a challenging issue. Table 9 gives two video traces. The display rates for MPEG and JPEG videos are 24 and 30 frames/sec, respectively.

Movie name	Length (min)	No. of frames	Ave. Rate (Kbps)	Peak rate (Kbps)	Size (Mbytes)
Star Wars	121	174055	374	4447	339.42
Sleepless in Seattle	120	181457	2275	3988	1719.74

Table 9 Display rates for two movies

Video proxy servers can be used to assist the end-to-end video delivery to alleviate the burden of WAN or LAN from the high bandwidth requirement and rate variability of video traffic. [49] propose a framework of staging portion of a video in proxy server to reduce the bandwidth requirement of WAN. In figure 17 proxy servers have been used to reduce network congestion and improve client access time on the Internet by caching passing data.

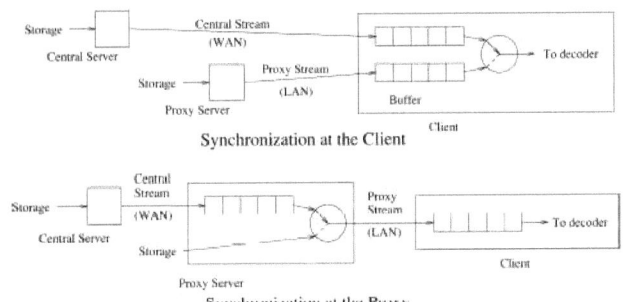

Figure 17 Two synchronization models for proxy servers used to reduce network congestion and increase Internet access [49]

The quality of the multimedia stream is based on the available network bandwidth between the proxy and the client. A client needs to access a portion of the video from a proxy server over a local area network (LAN) and the rest from a central server across a wide area network. The video delivery rate is shown to depends on the tradeoff between client buffer, storage requirement on the proxy serve and bandwidth requirement over LAN and WAN. Therefore large bandwidth over LAN becomes necessary to access video conferencing services. These services are now commercially available [50]

Digital Home

It is expected that data for audio, video, telephone, printing, will be transported through the home over a digital network [51]. Standards to enable the delivery of selected programming from cable set top boxes to DTV sets units IEEE1394 (as given in table10) have been approved by the Consumer Electronics Manufacturers Association (CEMA) and the Society of Cable and Telecommunication Engineers (SCTE).

Speed	Equipment
S 400 (500 Mbps)	Digital TV, PC, Printer, Camera
S 200 (250 Mbps)	D-VCR, CD Player, Audio Amplifier
S 100 (125 Mbps)	DV Camera

Table 10 IEEE standards for digital home [52]

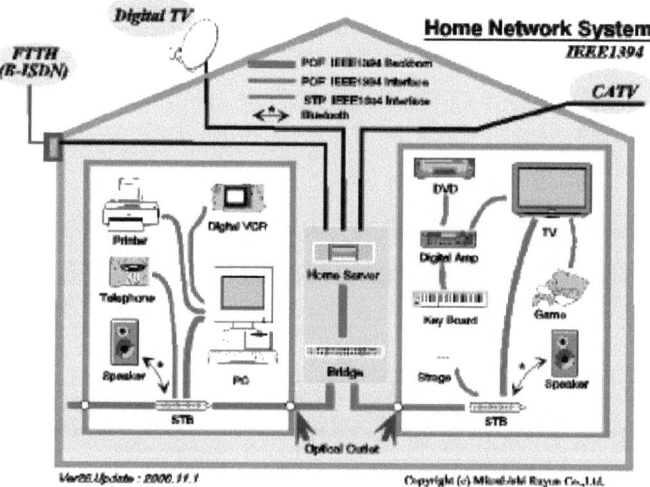

Figure 18 Digital home [53]

3.3 Market for POF Network

The network for the distances in the range of about 500m is called Fiber to the home (FTTH). LAN is divided into different segments. Ethernet in office LAN and home networks is a recent trend in most of the industrialized countries. In Japan [www.americasnetwork.com] research by KDDI, which entered the market last October, introducing bundled Internet, IP phone and TV services for just 6,500 yen ($65) a month, suggests that 70% of the users intend to move to FTTH. That is not surprising since FTTH offers much more speed for only $15-$30 more per month. FTTH in Japan is by far the least expensive in the world. The following figure 19 [54] shows FTTH growth in Japan.

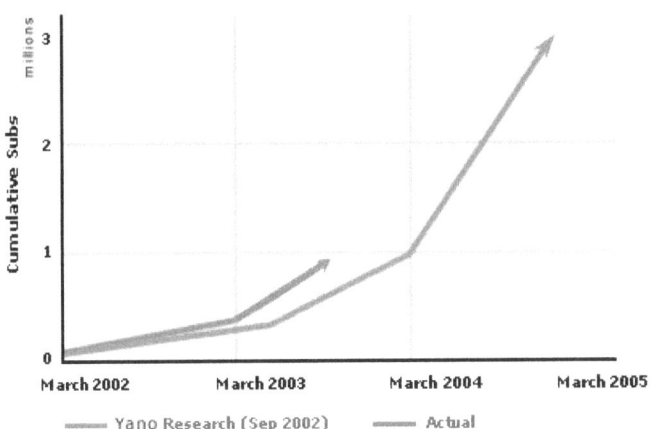

Figure 19 Forecast vs. real data by Japan's Ministry of Telecom [54]

The rapid deployment of FTTH in Japan is largely due to a strong competitive environment that is eroding incumbent local exchange carriers' (ILECs) revenues from plain old telephony service (POTS). NTT, the world's largest and fastest growing FTTH provider, has been among the first to recognize that ILECs' future is broadband. FTTH is the ultimate broadband medium, providing 1000 times the bandwidth of DSL. While reaching critical mass in Asia, equipment prices of FTTH are rapidly dropping, following the price curve of previous-generation broadband equipment such as DSL and cable modems. In Italy, Milan, Italy has one of the highest FTTH (fiber to the home) penetration rates in the world: 20% of home Internet connections are fiber [55]

In U.S.A. FTTH is not as rapidly deployed. It is left to "the market will show if the replacement of old cables with optical fibers is needed". However to date , USA is the biggest customer of FTTH [RVA] . Figure 20 illustrate this point.

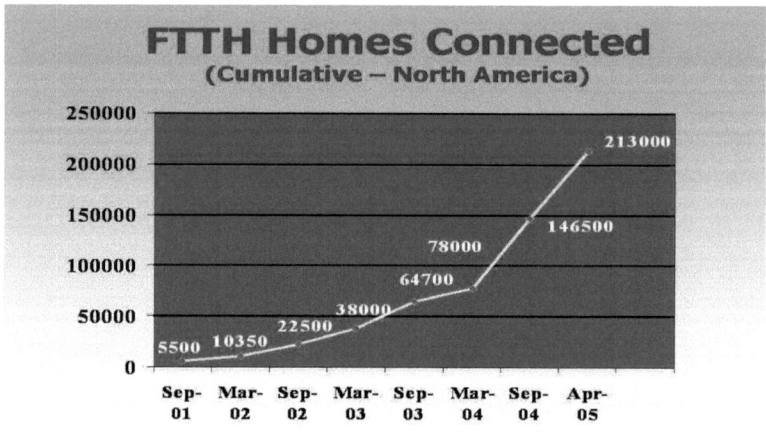

Figure 20 FTTH homes connected for North America [55]

Market researchers are predicting a total of 40Million high-speed connection by the end of 2005 [56] . Figure 21 maps the house hold penetration of high speed access (or FTTH network).

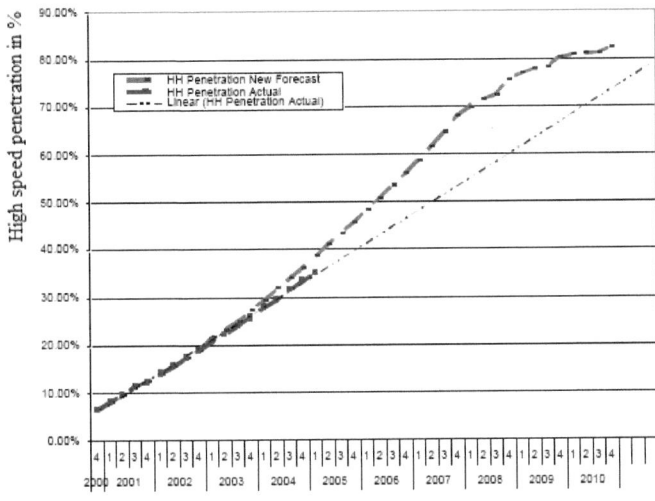

Figure 21 First quarter 2005 household penetration of high speed access [57]

This optimistic forecast suggests that by 2009 , 80% of the households in USA will have access to high speed if the linear growth will continue as from 2000 to 2005.

In conclusion, POF technology has been a developing technology. A lack of initial applications was in the beginning of the history of this technology, however it has the potential of being a low cost technology today (large-scale production in the auto industry have already prove that). The demand for high-speed and large capacity exist , because the new opportunities for consumer appliances has emerged due to the low cost of digital imaging and storage; applications in auto industry already exist. POF network market is not anymore a nice market, but a huge market.

Chapter 4 Transceiver technology

Basic elements of an optical fiber communication system include the fiber, transmitter (light –emitting diode (LED), laser (edge or vertical surface emitting), and the receiver (positive-intrinsic-negative (PIN) diode and avalanche photodetector (APD) detectors, optical preamplifiers, receiver electronics) . For the transceiver the figure of merit will be :

$$FOM = \frac{Speed}{Power*Cost}$$

Speed refers to the bit rate; Power refers to the output laser power as well as the lowest detectable power for the detector. The transceiver discussed in this thesis require bit error rate (BER) equal to 10^-12.

BER

Light signal with power P and B is bit rate
#Photons/sec=P/hv
Ave # Photons within one bit interval = N = P/(hvB)
Given N photons are sent, the probability of reading n photons within one bit interval is $P(n) = e^{-N} \dfrac{N^n}{n!}$ where $N = \dfrac{P}{hvB}$
Bit error rate (BER) = probability of sending a 0-bit* a 1-bit being read when 0-bit is sent + probability of sending a 1-bit* a 0-bit being read when 1-bit is sent
Prob. Of sending 1-bit = Prob. Of sending 0-bit = 0.5
Prob. Of 0-bit being read when a 1-bit is sent = $p(0) = e^{-N}$
Prob. Of 1-bit being read when a 0-bit is sent = 0

$$BER = \frac{e^{-P/hvB}}{2}$$

and the number of photons required for a given BER is

$$N = \ln(2 \cdot BER)$$

It requires 27 photons for a 10^-12 BER.

Discussion of the wavelength is the first thing to discuss regarding the design of the transceiver.

4.1 Wavelength

To have efficient transmission with POF, wavelengths that match minimum attenuation values of POF are choosen. Figure 22 shows attenuation versus wavelength for a) PMMA and b)(PF) POF.

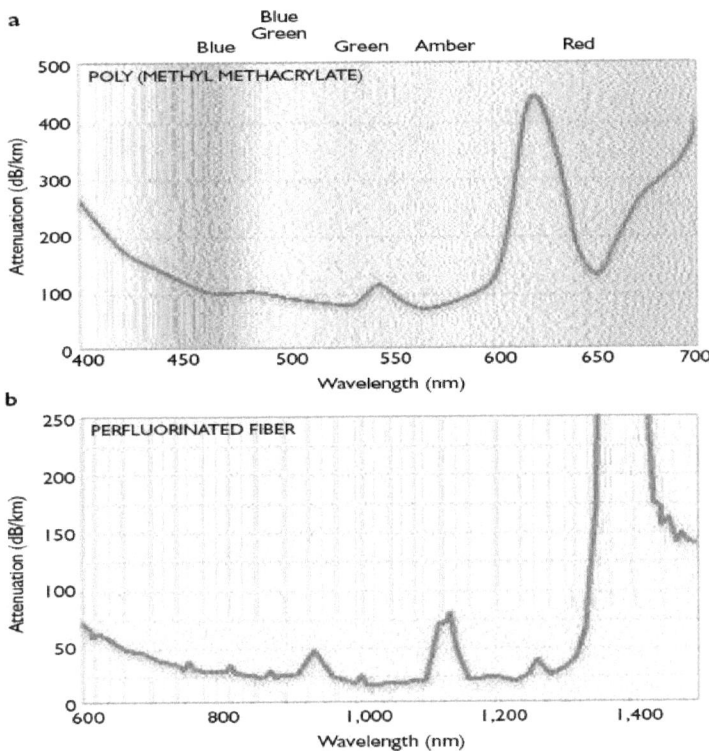

Figure 22 Attenuation versus wavelength for PMMA(a) and PF POF (b) [2]

The low loss window for PMMA fibers are near 520,570and 650nm and for PF POF near 850, 980nm, therefore to create efficient optical system, sources of light should be chosen in those ranges. Next section will talk about light sources.

4.2 Transmitter

The use of semiconductor diodes (SD) dominates the transmitter today because SD are very small (smaller than 1mm3), very fast switching times (a few nm), high efficiency (over 50%), long service life and good reliability , large application temperature range and economical to manufacture and process.

4.2.1 LED

LED's are forwarded biased positive-negative junctions, where carrier recombination results in spontaneous emission at a wavelength corresponding to the energy gap. The internal efficiency of LED can be as high as 60% , [59]
LEDs are often glued to the layer package face down on the metal carrier. The substrate is transparent so it does not effect the radiation. From a high radiance LED several milliwatts may be radiated, however the radiation is over a wide angular range making coupling loss a problem. LED radiation has a large spectral width, determined by thermal effects. At 850nm, LED-s tend to be intramodal dispersion limited[60] . Coupling light is done usually by having a lens because of the large angle of radiation for LED. Some of the commercial available LED's today are LEDs that enhance emission efficiency via a high output power LED chip mounted in a reflector (mirror) at the package base with peak emission wavelengths that range from 660 nm to 940 nm and 1300 nm to 1650 nm are commercially available. [www.sales.hamamatsu.com]. Green LEDs at a wavelength of 520nm are reported to have been used successfully in POF transmission for about 100m[58].

4.2.2 Laser

The first semiconductor laser diode to radiate continuously at room temperature was achieved in 1970 [61] Laser-s evolution continued in the 1990 with the advent of optical amplifiers. Population inversion between the ground and excited states in a laser results in stimulated emission. In edge emitting laser the radiation is guided within the active region of the laser and is reflected back at the faces; in vertical surface emitting lasers (VCSEL) reflection is from internal mirrors grown within the semiconductor structure.
Figure 23 shows a cross sectional view of the oxidized GaAs VCSEL

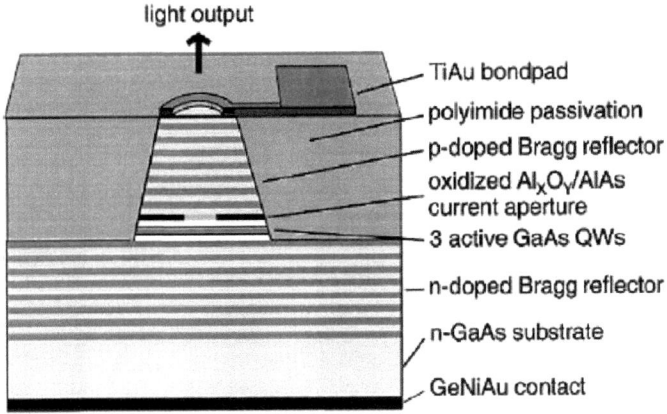

light output

TiAu bondpad
polyimide passivation
p-doped Bragg reflector
oxidized Al$_x$O$_y$/AlAs current aperture
3 active GaAs QWs
n-doped Bragg reflector
n-GaAs substrate
GeNiAu contact

Figure 23 Cross sectional view of the oxidized GaAs VCSEL [62]

Laser radiation is confined to a much narrower angular rang than for an LED, which means higher efficiency in coupling. A laser has a series of advantages compare to LED. Because of the stimulated emission in lasers , the external efficiency is higher; the high carrier density results in high modulation speed. Resonance frequency was less than 1GHz in early lasers; today frequencies up to 10 GHz [63] or 21.5-GHz modulation bandwidth of selectively oxidized InGaAs VCSEL's [64], are reported. Light is emitted from a considerably smaller surface in a smaller angle range than with LED. The laser wavelength is not determined by the semiconductor but by the resonant cavity properties. Also the use of selective oxidation for current confinement in VCSEL's has led to devices with extremely low threshold currents.[65] ,[66], [67]. Table 10 summarizes the comparison of LED and Laser.

	Output Power	Current	Coupled Power	Speed	Bandwidth	Wavelengths Available
LED	Linearly proportional to drive current	Drive current 50to 100mA	Medium	Slower	Moderate	0.6 to 1.65 µm
Laser	Proportional to current above threshold	Threshold Current 5 to 40mA	High	Fast	High	0.78 to 1.65 µm

Table 10 Comparison of LED and Laser

4.2.3 Low Cost Light Source for POF Optical System

One approach to lower the cost of the POF optical system is to reduce the cost of the light sources. As said above, several types of light sources can transmit data through POF, including light-emitting diodes (LEDs), edge emitting laser diodes, and vertical-cavity surface-emitting laser (VCSEL) diodes. To date, POF system using conventional POF uses Laser Emitted Diodes (LED) as light sources at 650nm wavelength. For PMMA table 11 gives the ability of various light sources.

Wavelength, nm	Light-emitting diodes	Surface-light-emitting diodes	Laser diodes	Vertical-cavity surface-emitting diodes	Resonant-cavity light-emitting diodes	Near-resonant-cavity light-emitting diodes
530	Yes	No	No	No	No	No
570	Yes	No	No	No	Samples	No
650	Yes	Yes	Yes	Samples	Samples	No
Modulation	250 Mbps	250 Mbps	4 Gbps	1 Gbps	600 bps	1.3 Gbps

Table 11   The ability of various light sources for PMMA [68]

The main difficulty of fabricating such devices is due to some inherent material limitations at 650nm such as a lower index contrast in Al GaAs/Al As-Bragg layers, and a weak electron confinement in AlGaInP/GaInP hetero-structures. The applications are generally consumer oriented so cost is number one priority. VCSELs are faster than LEDs, and more efficient and cheaper than edge-emitting lasers. Low-cost, high-performance, standardized serial optical links for distances up to several hundred meters based on VCSELs, such as Gigabit Ethernet, are now commercially available. "Error-free" transmission at 1 Gb/s has been reported through 50-meter of graded-index POF using the planar VCSEL consists of an AlGaInP/GaInP [69].

Vertical Cavity Surface Emitting Lasers (VCSELs) are the most commonly used light source for data communications at 850nm over multimode optical fiber, because these lasers are much cheaper to produce. Since the inception of the IEEE and Fibre Channel standards for high-speed data communications in 1997, more than 30 million VCSELs have been shipped into this application [70].   Figure 24 is a plot of the total 850nm VCSEL port shipments since commercialization in 1996. This data is taken from various marketing reports and industry surveys [71]

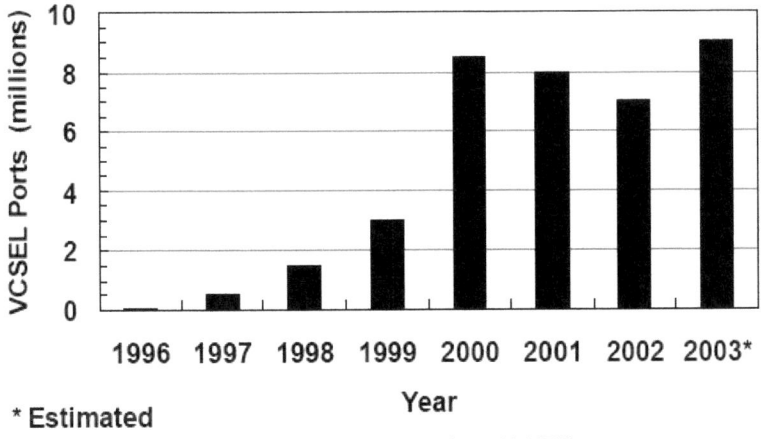

Figure 24 VCSEL shipments since 1996 [71]

The ideal situation would be if semiconductor lasers would integrate with silicon based circuits, then the cost of the light source would come down to almost 0$. Section 5.2.1 discusses this in details.

4.3 Receiver

4.3.1 Photodetector technology

Fiber optic systems generally use PIN or APD photodetectors. In avalanche photodetectors (APD), a large reverse voltage accelerates carriers, causing additional carriers by impact ionization. As a result current is proportional to current gain of the APD. Even though this can result in an improvement in receiver sensitivity, in an APD receiver additional shot noise is present because of the excess noise of the avalanche gain process. In PIN photodetectors absorption of light is done in the intrinsic region. Carriers generated there are swept out by the reverse-bias field. This results in a photocurrent that is proportional to the incident optical power. PIN will be discuss in more details in this thesis.

The main characteristics of the photodetcor are :

- Quantum efficiency

Quantum efficiency η gives an expression for the percentage of incoming photons that are actually absorbed by the detector material.

$$\eta = (1 - R)\xi(-\exp(-\alpha w))$$

Optimization of quantum efficiency includes:

(1-R) represent the effect of reflection at the surface of the device. Reflection can be reduced by the use of antireflection coatings.

Factor ξ is the fraction of electron hole pairs that successfully avoid recombination at the material surface and contribute to the useful photocurrent. Surface recombination can be reduced by careful material growth.

$\exp(-\alpha W)$ represents the fraction of the photon flux absorbed in the bulk of the material. The PIN should have a sufficiently large value of width of depletion region, to maximize this factor. α - absorption coefficient of depletion region. Based on figure 25 silicon detectors are practical for 850nm wavelengths. For 10Gbit/s applications quantum efficiency of a PIN detector need to be above 70% and for 1 to 3 Gbit/s 30% quantum efficiency is required.

- Responsivity

Responsivity is an expression of the current produced in the detector for a given signal power and is one of the most important parameters in characterizing a detector.

$$R = I / P_o \ (A/W)$$

48

Responsivity can be calculated from following formula:

$$R = \eta q / h\nu$$

Where η is quantum efficiency, q = electron charge, h = Planck's constant, ν = the frequency of incoming light

- Speed

Speed or as usually referred the bandwidth of the detector is determined by either the transit-time spread τ or the RC time constant. If bandwidth is limited by transit time then

$$\text{Bandwidth} = 1 / \tau tr$$

Photons that are absorbed create an electron-hole pair by promoting an electron in the valance band into the conductance band. The electrons and holes travel to the electrodes swept by the reverse-bias field. The electrons travel faster than holes. τ_{tr} is the time it takes for a hole (being the slowest moving charge carrier) to drift one half the depletion region, and can be expressed as;

$$\tau_{tr} = \text{width of intr.} / v_{drift}$$

Response time can also be limited by the resistance and capacitance of the detector. Once the electrons and holes are creates, they must travel through the semiconductor material to the electrodes, then they must travel through some distance until they reach the connector wire.

$$\text{Resistance} = L / (C * t * w)$$

L = length of detector, σ = conductivity, t = thickness, w = width

The receiver performance is conditioned from the capacitance of the photodiode and the receiver circuit

Conductivity is given as $C_3 = ne\mu$
n = number of carriers/cm , e = electron charge, μ = mobility

The bandwidth of the detector could be increased by making the depletion layer thinner. This would reduce the difference in transit time between electrons and holes. However for efficient coupling, means surface area of the diode needs to be as large as possible. One approach to bring capacitance as low as possible is through metal-semiconductor-metal (MSM) photodiode, however MSM cannot be made in a standard CMOS process, meaning cost goes up.
The speed of the detector at wavelength 850nm can be increased also if Ge is used instead of Si. The electron mobility on Ge is 3900 cm2/V-s while the electron mobility of Si is 1350 cm2/V-s. Today Ge detector can be effectively grown on Si .The lattice mismatch

of Si to Ge is about 4%, resulting in a minimal lattice strain and associated defects. The bandgap energy of Ge is 0.66 eV for the indirect gap and 0.8 eV for direct gap. Absorption at the direct gap is desirable because the quantum efficiency is greater. Improving the geometry of design (like finger photodetector) have brought up the bandwidth of the photodetectors too.

- Low noise

Noise arises from thermal generation of electron hole pair is called shot noise

Noise arise from higher resistance at higher temperature is called thermal noise.

$$i_{n,thermal}^2 = \frac{2kTB}{R}$$

Noise power $N = i_{shot}^2 + i_{thermal}^2$

Usually Signal to Noise ratio is given in literature.

$$\frac{S}{N} = \frac{Power_{signal}}{Power_{noise}} = \frac{i_s^2}{i_n^2} = \frac{i_s^2}{i_{n,shot}^2 + i_{n,thermal}^2}$$

High quantum efficiency, speed, responsivity and low noise level are desirable for the receiver to achieve the requirements for the transceiver.

4.3.2 Photodetector Material

POF optical systems success depends in the ability to bring down the cost of its components. Silicon foundries are very well established which makes Si the preferred semiconductor material from the cost point of view. The receiver performance is conditioned from the capacitance of the photodiode and the receiver circuit. Electrical circuits can be fabricated, for example, in silicon or in GaAs. GaAs is a good absorber at 850 nm and it is possible to obtain a very fast response with the quantum efficiency reaching nearly one. High absorption coefficient will result in high quantum efficiency and responsivity; GaAs is also a direct bandgap material (efficient at generating photocarriers). It also has very high electron and hole mobility (Electron mobility for GaAs is 8500cm2/V-s and for Si is 1350cm2/V-s), which is ideal for very high-speed operations.The performance of the circuits is lower on Si compared to GaAs, however very high circuit densities can be achieved on Si, and at a lower cost, making it a preferred technology.

50

The detector on Si will take advantage of Si integrated circuitry that is more common and cheaper than other materials systems. To create an electron hole pair an incoming photon must have enough energy to raise an electron across the bandgap, $hf > E_{gap}$. For Si the bandgap is 1.1 eV so silicon detectors are the most practical detectors at wavelengths between 800nm and 900nm. Actually, responsivity maximum for Si occurs for wavelengths substantially shorter than the bandgap wavelength because Si is an indirect-gap material. The photon absorption transition therefore takes place from the valence band to conduction band states that typically lie well above the conduction band edge. Figure 25 shows the absorption coefficient and penetration depth for various semiconductors .

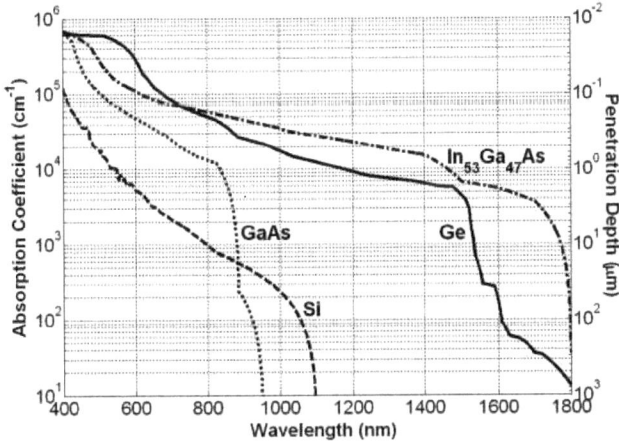

Figure 25 Absorption Coefficient and penetration depth for various semiconductors [25]

If one is looking for high speed (up to 10Gbitps) devices CMOS compatible than Ge becomes the material of choice for the receiver.

4.3.3 Ge- photodetector material for future applications of broad band optical communications

To date available LAN's applications are require at most 3Gbitps (video communication) speed. New applications will emerge as low cost transceivers and low loss plastic fibers are being addressed from the researchers. Most likely those future applications will require more speed (in the range of 10Gbps) than Si can offers. Among the semiconductors that offer higher speed than Si, are III-V semiconductors or Ge. As discussed in Chapter 6 , the cost of the transceiver is brought down drastically if the process flow is CMOS compatible. So the best material choice to keep the cost of the optical transceiver down and to increase the speed is Ge. Figure 26 illustrate this point.

51

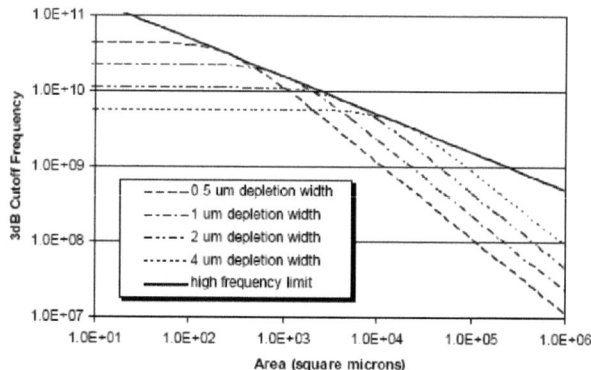

Figure 26 3dB cutoff frequency for Ge vertical PIN diodes used for detector design [25]

Ge detector can be effectively grown on Si. The lattice mismatch of Si to Ge is about 4%, The bandgap energy of Ge is 0.66 eV for the indirect gap and 0.8 eV for direct gap. The advantages of Ge in a photodetector compare to Si would be:

- Stronger absorption, which means higher sensitivity. Figure 27 gives absorption of Ge on Si [72]

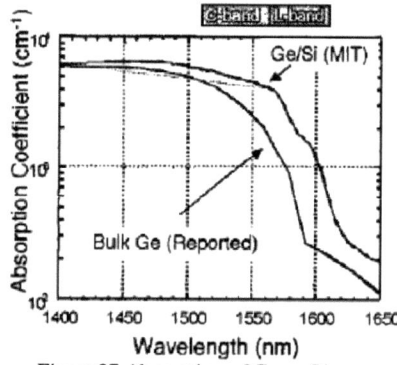

Figure 27 Absorption of Ge on Si

- Higher mobility (x 3 in bulk), therefore faster drift and diffusion

Bulk Ge has electron mobility of 3900 cm^2/V-sec and a hole mobility of 1900 cm^2/V-sec.

- The growth and fabrication process of Ge detector is compatible with CMOS processing and so can be monolithically integrated with CMOS circuits. CMOS circuits can be fabricated first on silicon substrate with some marked areas for germanium detector growth.

Photodetector on Ge are reported in [73] .SiGe pin-photodiodes (figure 28) were fabricated on thick graded (10% Ge per μm) buffers with a Ge content up to 100%. Growth of the thick graded buffer layers was performed by LEPECVD.[74]

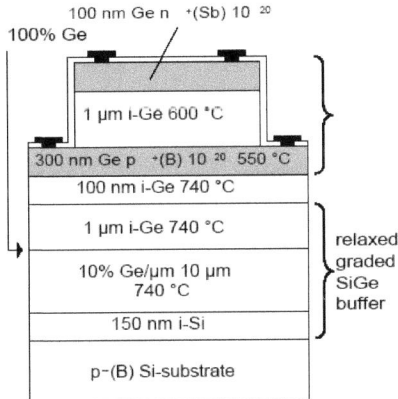

Figure 28 Cross section of the Ge on Si photodetector [74]

100% Ge photodiodes with an 1μm thick intrinsic zone are reported [75] to exhibit dc-photoresponsivities of 145mA/W at a wavelength of 1.3μm and 25mA/W at 1.55μm even at zero bias and an RC-limited 3dB opto-electrical bandwidth of 0.9GHz .
Summary of SiGe/ Si photodetectors (table12) in the NIR is given in [76]

Structure	Efficiency	Dark current	Notes
pure Ge pin	η_{ext}=40% @ λ=1.45μm	50mA/cm^2	
SiGe MQW photoconductor	η_{ext}=59% @ λ=1.3μm η_{int}=300% @ λ=1.3μm		dem. 200MB/s (25Km)
SiGe MQW pin waveguide	η_{int}=40% @ λ=1.3μm	7mA/cm^2	f_T=1GHz FWHM=300ps
SiGe MQW APD waveguide	η_{ext}=400% @ λ=1.3μm		dem 800MB/s (45Km)
SiGe MQW	η_{ext}=1% @ λ=1.3μm	60mA/cm^2	
SiGeC	η_{ext}=1% @ λ=1.3μm	7mA/cm^2	
SiGe MQW pin waveguide	η_{ext}=11% @ λ=1.3μm η_{int}=40% @ λ=1.3μm	1mA/cm^2	f_T=1.2GHz
SiGe SL pin	η_{ext}=25% @ λ=0.98μm	50μA/cm^2	f_T=10GHz
pure Ge pn diode	η_{ext}=12.6% @ λ=1.3μm	0.15mA/cm^2	
pin SiGeC	η_{ext}=2% @ λ=1.3μm	0.1mA/cm^2	
MSM Ge	η_{ext}=23% @ λ=1.3μm η_{int}=89% @ λ=1.3μm		f_T=0.5GHz

Table 12 Summary of SiGe/Si photodetectors in the NIR [76]

Ge photodetectors have been fabricated using Ge epilayers grown by the 2-step growth method and the responsivity spectra are found very close to an ideal responsivity curve [77] . Another approach to built Ge photodetectors on Si platform is used by [78] The authors presents a strain engineering of Ge photodetectors on Si. The band gap of the Ge film is shown to be engineered to 0.765eV (compared to 0.801eV of the unstrained Ge) as a result of 0.25% in-plane tensile strain, which corresponds to an effective photodetection range up to 1623nm and covers the whole L-band. A tensile strained Ge p-i-n diode with detection capability up to 1600nm has been demonstrated on Si platform .The responsivity of the device is significantly higher than the theoretical values of an un-strained Ge photodiode with the same film thickness .The responsivity of the tensile strained Ge photodetector at 1310,1550 and 1600nm are as high as 0.64A/W, 0.40A/W and 0.10A/W, respectively. High responsivity, Si-CMOS compatible devices like the ones mentioned above confirm that Ge is an ideal material for the future applications of broad band optical communications.

4.4 Coupling

One of the advantages of POF-based optical systems is that the requirements for alignment are much relaxed than in a silica-based optical system, because of the large dimensions of POF. However to improve coupling several methods are used from lenses to guiding holes [105]This section will describe the possible advantages that using POF offers in coupling light from the fiber to the receiver and from the transmitter to the fiber. Light diverges at a rather large angle as is comes out of the light source. Fiber pigtail is a prealigned length of fiber that can be spliced or connected to the fiber in the field. The alternative to using a fiber pigtail is the use of a microlens with a graded index, however pigtail coupling minimizes the coupling loss and is the preferred method for POF.

Because POF has a larger diameter compare to silica fiber the alignement and coupling is easier. Coupling of light from a light source can be done through embedment of the source and drive electronics into the connector housing (Figure 29), such as for transceivers used in automotive and consumer products.

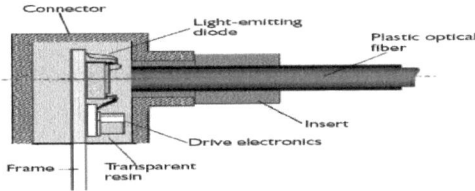

Figure 29 Connector, light source and POF fiber interfaced together [2]

Direct coupling of VCSELs to POF can be done using guide holes patterned in a thick photoresist as shown in figure 30 [45]

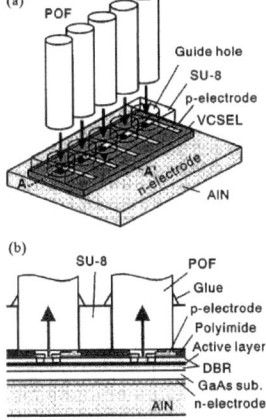

55

Chapter 5   Si Integration: Path to Cost Reduction

If all components of an optical transceiver are available commercially discrete
components what is the need of photonics on silicon or integration?
In the section 3.2.2. properties of silicon that affect its optical performance were discuss.
The speed of electronics based on Si has reached cut off frequency 130GHz which
would allow operation up to 45GHz [79] still devices based on III-V compounds are
ahead in speed. Optical transceiver designed for POF is going to be used by residential
customers. Technological performance and cost are going to determine the future path
that this transceiver will take. Sufficient performance is needed, however only low cost
will make the transceiver to succeed in market. Si pass the test of sufficient performance.
The following sections will discuss the cost benefits that Si offers for the transceiver and
also report the level of integration to date.

5.1 Photonics in silicon

III-V elements (InP, GaAs) offer excellent performance for the optical
transceiver. Much faster devices can be built on III-V's than in Si because their electron
mobility is much higher than the electron mobility of Si. However researchers haven't
stop looking for ways to built the transceiver in Si because of the cost advantages that Si
offers.

- Si is the dominant material in microelectronics today because Si foundries are
  very well establish. Si which is widely available, can be easy to handle and to
  manufacture and shows very good thermal and mechanical.
- The industry of Si would not be the same if the properties of SiO2 would not be
  as excellent as they are. Native oxide of silicon, SiO2, is not only an excellent
  insulator, but also an effective diffusion barrier and has a very high etching
  selectivity with respect to Si.
- Si has been the most studied semiconductor, at least the last 60 years, therefore a
  single dominating processing technology, CMOS, exist for more than 95% of the
  whole market of semiconductor chips[80]. Cost per bit is much reduced in Si as
  the integration of more and more devices (55000000 in Pentium) on larger and
  larger silicon wafers has been taken place. Figure 31 shows the evolution of the
  number of transceivers in a single central processing unit vs. the year [81]

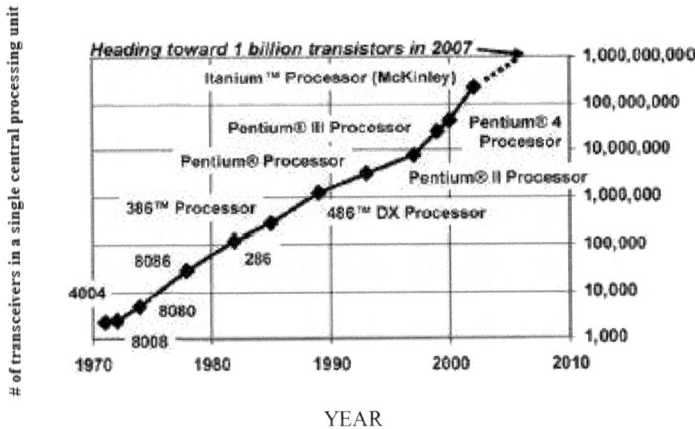

Figure 31 Number of transceivers in a single central processing unit vs. the year [81]

5.2 Integrated transceiver

Cost reduction through integration has been the path that the microelectronic technology successfully has taken. Integration, if would be done in photonics, would reduce the cost of packaging that actually counts for 70 to 80% of the total cost of the devices [25].

As concluded from [82] integration will ease of use of the device by making the device more user friendly than they are today and provide a level of interface management for the customer. Lowering manufacturing cost will come from integration since elimination of the cleaving process (for active devices to improve yields and reducing the number of fiber splices required) will happen. Packaging cost will be reduced because less hermetically sealed packages are needed. Integration of the device will enable components and modules that require less real estate than their current discrete equivalents. Integrated devices will be more energy efficient, in terms of communication signals between functions- including both RF and optical.

However with integration complication of the processing increases and several barriers (as described in more details in [82]) have emerged. First barrier is lower yield for the process as integration takes place as well as materials process capability, process integration hierarchy, polarization diversity, optical loss and heterogeneity.

It was predicted in the early 1990 that silicon based optoelectronics would be a reality before the end of the century and all but silicon laser have already been demonstrated[83] Optical component markets at $1.5 billion (US) are expected to reach $2.4 billion by 2009[84]. The world-wide market for integrated active optical products at $1.1 billion in 2003 will grow to $1.5 billion in 2009 [85]

57

Laser Integration : A laser is needed to have high speed optical transceiver. Several strategies are followed to build a laser in Si [86]. A weighting of each of those approaches is given in [87] . Basically, they differ both for spectral region of emission and for the physics behind. Figure 32 shows a schematic sketch of the various strategies that are currently followed to build a silicon laser.

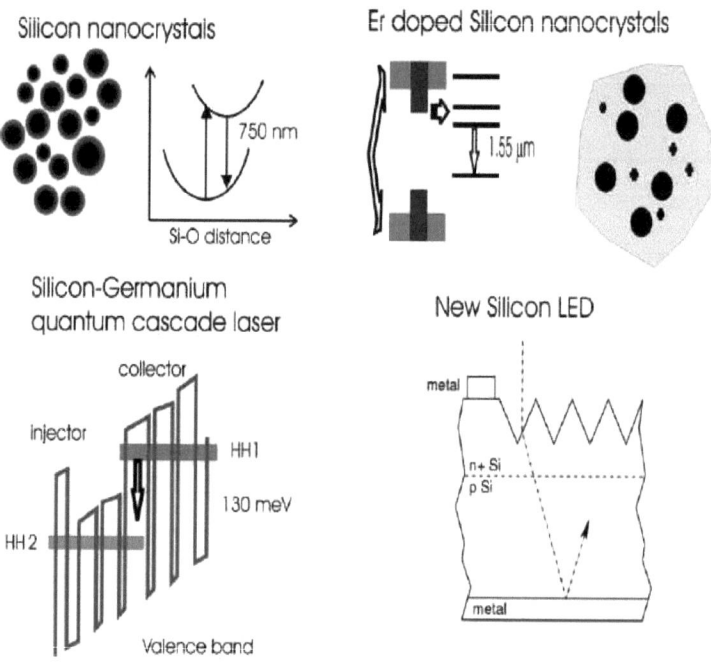

Figure 32 Strategies to build silicon laser

Monolithic integration of room-temperature cw GaAs-AlGaAs lasers on Si substrates via relaxed graded GeSi buffer layers is another approach toward integration[88] . Also from [89] another step toward integration is realized: Si:Er photons from LED directly modulated by MOSFET driver.

Receiver Integration: Receiver need to convert the optical signal at 850nm into electrical signal by using silicon based photodetectors. High speed (up to 8 Gb s−1) monolithically integrated silicon photoreceivers at 850 nm have been fabricated by using 130 nm CMOS technology on a SOI wafer [90]. Silicon integrated photoreceivers able to detect signals with a high responsivity of 0.46 A W−1 at 3.3 V for 845 nm light and 2.5 Gb s−1 data rate are also reported on [91]. A 200 GHz Ge photdetector on Si platform that covers a broad detection spectrum from 850-1600nm is reported [92]. PIN diode has been reported to be fabricated from tesile strained Ge epitaxial material with fully Si-CMOS compatible processes; at 0V bias the responsivity of the device at 850nm is 0.50A/W which can be further increased by 30% with antireflection coating. The high responsivity at 850nm enables on chip optoelectronic applications of the device. The device is reported to be fully compatible with Si CMOS technology, which enables monolithically integrated photodiodes with Si circuitry.

5.3 Silicon based waveguides

Silicon based waveguides are needed to be silicon compatible and should withstand normal microelectronics processing. When designing the waveguide one assesses parameters like index of refraction of the core material, its electro-optical effects, the optical losses and the transparency region. Different approaches have been followed to realize low optical loss waveguides, [93] :

- low dielectric mismatch structures (e.g. doped silica , silicon nitride or silicon oxynitride on oxide [94] , [95]
- differently doped silicon [96]
- high dielectric mismatch structures (e.g. silicon on oxide) [97]

Techniques like adiabatic tapers, V-grooves, and grating couplers have been proposed to improve optical loss. Figure 33 shows the schemes to couple the light from a fiber into a waveguide by using taper , grating coupler, or from a vaveguide into a photodiode by using a total internal reflection mirror

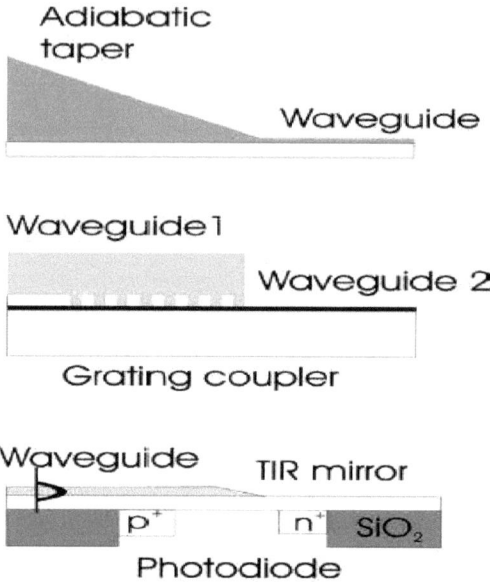

Figure 33 Schemes to couple the light from a fiber into a waveguide by using taper, grating coupler, or from a vaveguide into a photodiode by using a total internal reflection mirror.

Waveguides on Si substrate can be made from different materials like silica, silicon nitride or silicon oxynitride. SiON and Si3N4 can also be used for 850 and 650nm transmission. Silicon on silicon waveguides are very effective for realizing free-carrier injection active devices (e.g. modulators) as well as fast thermo-optic switches thanks to the high thermal conductivity of silicon. The downside of these waveguides is that scattering loss becomes extremely sensitive when high index contrast is increased or when bending radii is decreased as shown in figure 34.

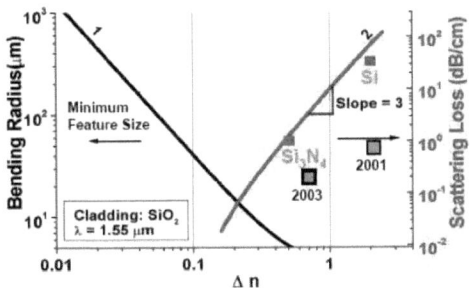

Figure 34 Bending radius and scattering loss as a function of index contrast, for Si based waveguides [97]

Unlike the size of the transistors on chip, the size of the waveguide is relatively large which doesn't allow the integration of large number of optical components in one chip. Figure 35 compare the cross sections of a CMOS chip with a silica waveguide

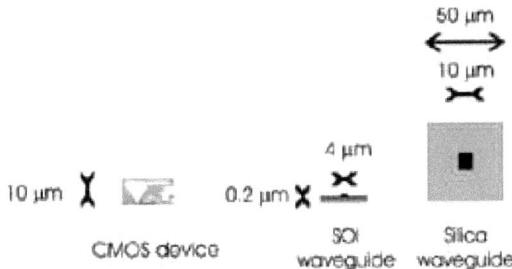

Figure 35 Cross sections of CMOS chip, SOI waveguide and silica waveguide.

If waveguides are done small then another problem, coupling efficiency to the fiber becomes evident. The nitride based waveguides are extremely flexible with respect to the wavelength of the signal light: both visible and IR. At the other extreme, silicon on insulator (SOI) or polysilicon based waveguides allow for a large refractive index mismatch and, hence, for small size waveguides in the sub-micrometer range. This allows a large number of optical components to be integrated within a small area. A number of photonic components in SOI such as directional couplers, dense WDM arrayed waveguide grating, Mach–Zehnder filters and star couplers have been demonstrated and commercialized [98],[99]

5.4 Silicon photonics integrated circuits

Hybrid integration of active components and silica-based planar lightwave circuits provides a full scheme for photonic component integration within a chip. Passive components are realized by using silica waveguides while active components are hybridized within the silica . Active components (laser diodes, semiconductor optical amplifiers and photodiodes) are flip-chip bonded on silicon terraces where the optical waveguides are also formed. By using this approach, various photonic components have been integrated such as multi-wavelength light sources, optical wavelength selectors, wavelength converters, all optical time-division multiplexers etc [100]

A full integrated optical system based on silicon oxynitride waveguides, silicon photodetectors and CMOS transimpedance amplifiers has been realized [101]. A compact, low cost WDM transceiver for the LAN has been reported also in [102] In this paper, a fully integrated transceiver is described in which four lasers, four detectors, a wavelength multiplexer, a wavelength demultiplexer, and all necessary electronics are contained within a duplex-connectorized module. The component technologies that enable the transceiver to be compact and low-cost are also described. Figure 36 shows an illustration of a half-inch wide WWDM transceiver module that is being developed at Agilent Laboratories for possible use in 10-GbE LAN applications. The proposed module is based on a printed circuit board with a ball-grid array electrical interface and an MT-RJ duplex fiber-optic connector interface.

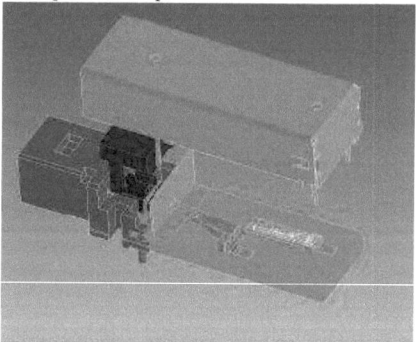

Figure 36Half-inch wide WWDM transceiver module

The authors have demonstrated 10-Gb/s data transmission across 300 m of multimode fiber using a compact WWDM transceiver design. The package design will also support a 10- km link distance over single-mode fiber. By using low-cost component technology, including an injection-molded plastic wavelength demultiplexer, reduced-specification DFB lasers, and compact planar waveguide technology, the cost of this module should be consistent with traditional LAN transceiver costs. This technology is ideally suited for the newly emerging 10-Gigabit Ethernet LAN market.

In conclusion, monolithic integration on III-V platform is mature today [103] . III-V platform offers faster devices, however POF optical transceiver is going to be a residential consumer device therefore sufficient performance is needed. The path to cost reduction is through integration of the devices on Si, to take advantages of Si-large scale integration and the high volume market offer by applications for LAN make possible cost reduction for the POF optical transceiver .

CHAPTER 6 COST MODEL

As has been described in preceding chapters, cost is now a driving force for the transceiver industry. From a technology point of view, the transceiver industry is working to reduce cost using three main approaches. The first is particularly aimed at POF transceivers, the latter two are generally applicable:

1. Moving from unidirectional to bidirectional devices

To date, only unidirectional transceivers exists on the market for POF. Such designs require not only additional packaging, but, most critically, double the length of fiber required for each connection. With a bidirectional design only one fiber is used to transmit *AND* receive the optical signal. As shown in Table 13, POF fiber is a dominant expense – for a 10m connection fiber cost could reach $200 for unidirectional designs. Removing the second fiber provides immediate savings.

Fiber 1, (PMMA)	$6/m
Fiber2, (perfluorinated)	$10/m
VCSEL (850nm)	$.93
LD	$3.70
Si PD	$2.19
TIA	$2.00

Table 13   Comparing the price of the components in an optical system

2. Better component manufacturing (cheaper substrate, larger wafer sizes)

Currently, transceivers on the market are built on III-V semiconductor platforms, typically on 4 inch or smaller wafers. The cost of one InP wafer 100mm with epitaxial layer is about $1000; one GaAs wafer 100mm costs $500. III-V elements offer higher speed for the transceiver however the cost of one silicon wafer 4inch, 8inch and 12 inch is respectively $26, $40,$1000. **Si** has been the most studied semiconductor, at least the last 60 years, therefore a single dominating processing technology, CMOS, exists for more than 95% of the whole market of semiconductor chips. As a result being able to manufacture the transceiver into Si brings significant cost savings.

3. Integration

Integration provides a number of performance and economic advantages as describe in more detail in Sections 5.2, 5.3 and 5.4. Economically speaking, the largest benefit from integration arises from reducing the approximately 70% of cost that comes from packaging. However, integration also brings yield down because of the requisite more complicated processing. As such, determining whether integration provides cost savings requires a detailed analysis of a specific case. To give the answer to this question in the context of a bidirectional transceiver, three different designs were modeled using a process based cost model developed at MIT.

6.1 Different transceiver designs

In this thesis the impact of the design choices on the cost has been studied for three different transceivers. Design #1 considers discrete components and discrete subassembled packages; Design # 2. considers discrete components, where only the receiver is subassembled[1]; and Design # 3. is monolithically integrated device and package. A schematic of a discrete transceiver design (as in design #1) is given in Figure 37, showing the key components modeled [104]. The transceiver often consists only of the laser and the detector, each sealed in a TO-can and then incorporated into a metal box. The leads from the laser and detector subassemblies are connected to the appropriate electronics that drive the laser and manipulate the incoming data.

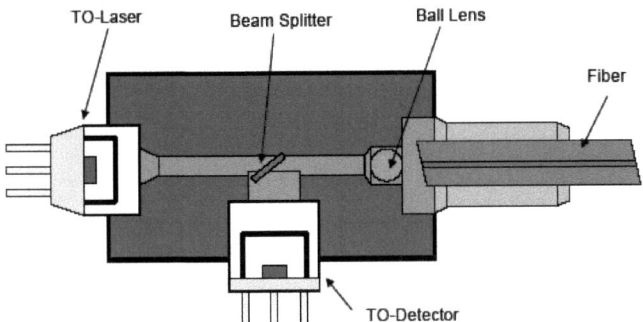

Fig 37 Discrete transceiver schematic. The laser and the detector are separately manufactured and hermetically sealed in a TO-can. The TO-cans are then integrated into a box along with a beam splitter to separate the incoming light and a lens used to focus the laser light into the fiber.

In design #1 and #2 the light source can be LED of VCSEL; their comparison is given in table 10. Design #3 has VCSEL as the light source .
.[1] Design 2 also differs from Design 1 in that it assumes that no additional lens are required within the package

.

6.2 Discrete design or integrated design (from cost of manufacturing/area point of view)?

The first thing to consider when starting the cost analysis of any semiconductor component is the size of the wafer. Three different size Si-substrates exist on the market: 4 inch ($26), 8 inch($40) and 12inch. 8 inch wafers are dominantly used in today's fabs due to their area/cost advantage. As such, an 8 inch wafer is used in the cost model for this analysis. The PD and TIA are the components that consume the largest area on the wafer. The receiver PD and transimpendance amplifier (TIA) are fabricated discretely in the first and second design. The simplest way to compare cost of manufacturing discrete or integrated photodiodes and TIA-s is to compare the cost of manufacturing per area. The products and processes modeled for this thesis do not require special equipment or very long processing compared to the TIA (cf. process flow in Appendix A). To calculate cost per area one should take in consideration cost divided by the good die area produced per year.

- Size of the die for PD   -- 2x2mm^2,
- Size of the die for TIA   -- 2x2mm^2.
- Size of the die in the integrated case -- 2x3mm^2.

As such, the integrated component would require 33% less die area compared to producing the two components separately. Obviously, monolithic integration is favored from the point of view of requiring less die area. However this is only a rough estimation. With integration not only the area of the devices changes, but also the level of complexity which means the yield of the processes changes. A more detailed analysis counting for the changes that come with integration as mentioned above is done through process based cost modeling.

6.3 Impact of line utilization on cost

The manufacturing of the optical transceiver is likely to require only a portion of any given foundry capacity. Therefore, different levels of dedication for production lines are considered in the model. Results from the cost model for the unit cost of the device when line dedication to transceiver is varied are presented on table 15. During the calculation it is assumed that the fab operates at 200,000 units per year.

% of line dedication	Design 1		Design 2		Design 3	
	PV=200,000	PV=50,000	PV=200,000	PV=50,000	PV=200,000	PV=50,000
All dedicated	$39.94	$48.72	$37.61	$44.08	$82.9	$305.21
All not dedicated	$36.75	$37.77	$34.99	$35.15	$7.97	$8.09
Investment weighted utilization	1.15	0.22	1.17	0.20	0.12	0.02

Table 15 Results for the unit cost for different line dedication

Based on the results presented on table 15, the unit cost of the integrated device is extremely high if line of production is dedicated to it. To illustrate the point, the range of the unit cost is increased almost 10 times for design #3, if it is calculated as 100% dedicated and 0% dedicated. One way that the industry is trying to solve this problem is to share the platform across products and increasing capability to run multiple products on a single line.

As mentioned above, during the calculations regarding the effect of line production percentage dedicated to the transceiver, is decisive in cost of the unit. The percentage of utilization of line production depends on the number of units manufactured per year. At a production volume 50,000 units per year the investment weighted utilization of the production line jumps to 2.1% ,compare to 0.5% utilization at 40,000 units. This increase of utilization is reflected on the cost reduction for the transceivers manufactured at production volumes above that critical number as shown in figure 38.

6.2 Sensitivity of unit cost to annual production volume

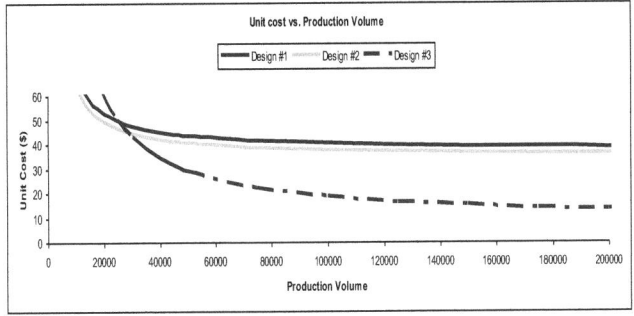

Figure 38 Unit Cost Sensitivity to Annual Production Volume

As can be seen from the figure 38 , for design#1 and #2 production volumes above 30,000 units per year are critical to reach economies of scale; for design #3 economies of scale are achieved for production volumes above 50,000 units per year. After that production volume (PV) for every 5000 units increase on PV the unit cost is reduced only 1%. Design #1 is the most expensive choice for production volumes above 30,000 units per year. Design #3 becomes the least expensive device for production volumes above 30,000 transceiver per year. Production volume equal to 30,000 units per year is the point where the integrated device becomes cheaper for the yields entered in the PBCM. To explain this switch in cost between the designs a cost breakdown by fixed and variable cost is needed. The cost breakdown by variable and fixed cost is given in figure 39 at PV= 50,000 and figure 40 at PV=200,000units . In the following figure, costs are grouped into: Materials(including purchased packaging components) , Labor (direct and indirect, both with benefits, but not managerial costs), Energy, Equipment and Other Fixed (Building's cost, maintenance, overhead).

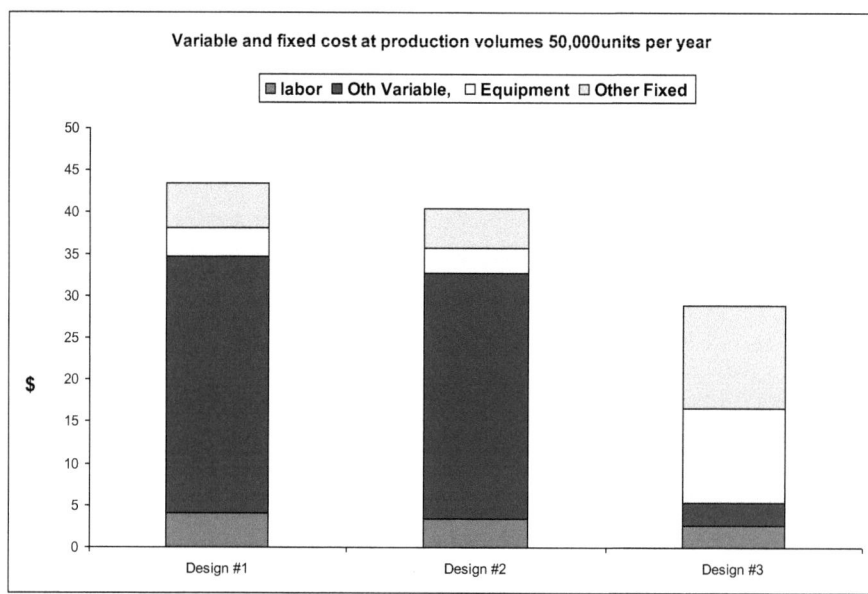

Figure 39 Variable and Fixed cost breakdown per unit cost at 50,000 units per year

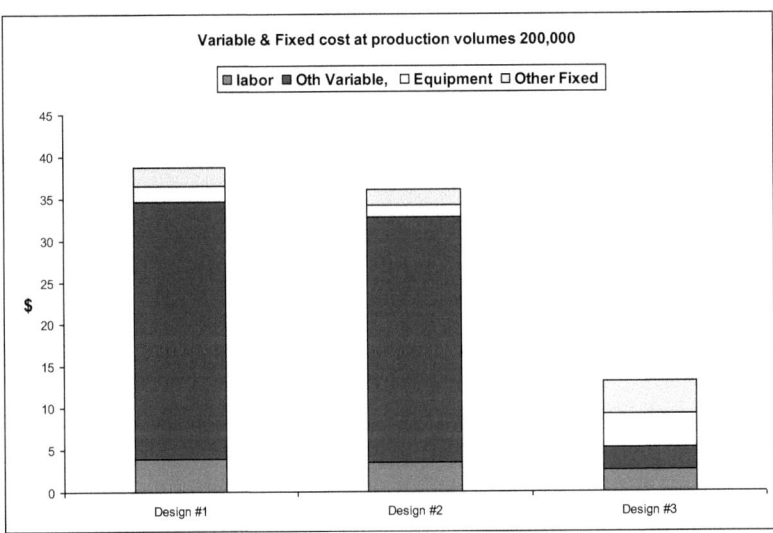

Figure 40 Variable and Fixed cost breakdown per unit cost at 200,000 units per year.

The main cost for design #3 comes from the fixed cost. As the PV increases above 100,000 units per year fixed cost per unit lowers for design #3 so it becomes cheaper then $20

The importance of reaching economies of scale as explained in this section will be followed by the discussion of yield on the following section because if the yield is improved than unit cost corresponding to the production volume will change .

6.3 Yield

Yield is measured throughout the manufacturing line, during wafer processing, wafer finishing and wafer test. For each of the designs the total yield is given as follows in Table 16

Design #	Yield
1	86%
2	87%
3	86% back end, 38% front end, 32% total

Table 16 Total yield given for different designs

As it can be seen from Table 16 , total yield drops sharply for design #3 .Total yield is determined from the yield of specific step during processing. Figure 39 gives the yield for the steps that impact the most total yield.

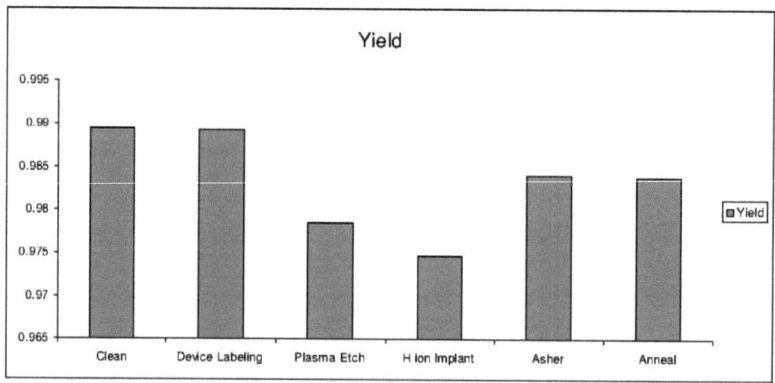

Figure 39 Yield of the steps that impact the most total yield during processing

Critical yield steps-Etching
A very critical yield step is via etch on the backside of the wafer to form ground contacts to the front or other etch processes. The hole needed for the contacts has the dimensions 10μm wide x 100μm deep. A highly anisotropic etch is needed to create a hole that is

uniform throughout the wafer. Even though the yield result for the integrated transceiver is discouraging, one should remember that limiting yield steps during packaging are saved when PD & TIA are manufactured in the same die.

Improvements to the yield of etching and also the the yield of growth and deposition processes increase the total yield of manufacturing to 35% (compare to 32% that is actually incorporated in the model). This higher yield results in lower cost for the transceiver from $13.135 at 32%yield into $12.96 for 35%yield.

As explained in [103] yield during dicing is a limiting factor for the commercially available photodiode build on GaAs or InP , however for our photodiodes build on Si or Ge because of the larger dimensions of the photodiode this process is not yield limiting anymore.

6.4 Cost breakdown by driving processes

From the above section is clear that to achieve a low cost transceiver economy of scale is necessary, as well as improvement of yield in specific processes. This section will give the cost breakdown by process to identify the cost driving processes. Focusing the development resources in the cost dominant areas helps the industry to lower the cost more efficiently. Driving cost processes are grouped in : Package back end, Test, Assembly Backed end, Lithography, Other Front , Growth/ Deposition and optical sub assembly processes. The results from the cost model for each design are in figure 41   .

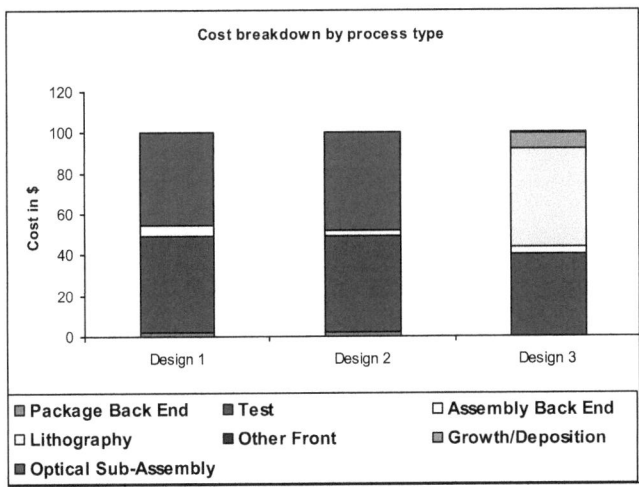

Figure 41   Comparison of cost breakdown by process type for all three designs.

The conclusions drawn from the analysis based on the cost breakdown by process are :

- The main cost for the discrete design #1 comes from
Assembly back end (58.6%) , Growth and deposition (12.2 %) , optical subassembly (20.5%)
- The main cost for the discrete design #2 comes from assembly back end (66%) and from growth and deposition (25%)

- In design # 3, optical subassembly & assembly back end have near zero cost, however the test cost is up to 6.8 %, and the cost of growth/ deposition process is increased to 45.89% of the total cost of the device.

- For design #1 and #2, cost savings would come from improvement in the assembly back end or subassembly cost, while for design #3 cost savings depends on realizing low cost assembly and from improvement in the growth/deposition process.

CONCLUSIONS

Currently the optical industry is trying to improve the optical network for short distances through several approaches.

1. Plastic optical fiber offers better performance than copper fibers and lower cost comparing to silica fibers. Low loss POF have been fabricated and commercialized. Because of the low cost advantage and increasing performance, POF has become the choice for Gigabit Ethernet applications in customer premises and local area networks.

2. Realizing a bidirectional transceiver
Cost reduction is the key for the future development of optoelectronic (OE) components, mostly driven by upcoming large volume applications. One approach is targeting a **bi-**directional transceiver because using bidirectional transceiver reduces in half the amount of fiber used compare to unidirectional transceiver in the optical network. .

3. Transitioning to a Si or Ge/Si platform
Creating an optical receiver within a Si or Ge material platform has huge advantages in terms of cost compared to a receiver in InP or GaAs (cost of the last ones is given in [103]). Having a transceiver manufactured through CMOS processes, leverages well known batch processes during component fabrication, and should reduce overall module fabrication cost.

4. Discrete or integrated
Although the efforts to lower the package cost remain useful, the results from the PBCM show that only when production volumes are above 30,000 units/year (critical to achieve economies of scale), the cost of the integrated transceiver is lower than the cost of the discrete one. Significant cost drop, below $20 is possible only for integrated transceiver at production volumes above 100,000 units per year.
Given that global markets for the transceiver is not more than 50,000 units per year, to reach economies of scale, firms are facing now a lack of demand. One way to increase the volume production for the transceiver would be to look at the fiber to the home (FTTH) installation. Today FTTH systems are design to provide more bandwidth than required from the customer point of view. The systems are designed to be upgraded (in case more bandwidth is required) through software and not through replacing components. Increase in demand for transceiver manufacturers is not likely to happen once initial deployment is complete; the replacement driver will be equipment failure and replacement, as opposed to technology upgrade [106] . The other options than is overseas demand for the optical transceiver. Also the approach toward the unidentified market would contribute to high production volumes. The unidentified market is considered the installation of an optical transceivers in home entertainment applications, although it is not being used at the moment from the customer. If transceivers were found in every new TV or DVD production would rapidly reach the necessary economies of scale. If yield of the etching processes are improved then the cost of the integrated transceiver drops even more, which makes the transceiver affordable from the customer point of view in every device like PC, Printer ect. With the huge market in front of the optical transceiver the integrated device becomes the choice for higher performance, and lower cost.

References:

[1] Diwakar Agarwal, "OPTICAL INTERCONNECTS TO SILICON CHIPS USING SHORT PULSES" PH.D thesis,Stanford University, September 2002]
[2] Paul Polishuk,, Industrial physicist , 2000
[3] Beach Communications
[4] W.Daum, J. Krauser, P.E.Zamzow, O.Zieman, "Polymer Optical Fibers for Data Communication", Springer 2000
[6] David G. Cunningham, William G. Lane, " Gigabit Ethernet Networking", Macmillan Technology Series, ISBN: 1-57870-062-0,1999
[7] Rich Seifert: "Gigabit Ethernet", Addison-Wesley, 1998]
[8] Ronny Bockstaele, "Fabrication of a low-cost module for Gigabit Ethernet transceivers",January,2004, Belgium
[9] www.RHK.com
[10] Zeadally;Zhang, ENABLING GIGABIT NETWORK ACCESS TO END USERS; PROCEEDINGS OF THE IEEE, VOL. 92, NO. 2, FEBRUARY 2004.
[11] Shuntaro Yamazaki, Minoru Shikada, C&C Media Research Laboratories, NEC corporation, Miyazaki Miyamaeku Kawasaki Kanagawa; POF for high-speed PC and home networks OFC '98 Technical Digest ,Japan
[12] Chikafumi Tanaka, Progress of perflurionated GI-POF; Porc.27th Eur. Conf. on Opt. Comm.(ECOC'01 - Amsterdam)
[13] H.P.A. v.d. Boom, P.K. van Bennekom, L.J.P. Niessen, A.M.J. Koonen, and G.D. Khoe; Gigabit Ethernet Transmission Experiments using GI-POF; COBRA Institute, Eindhoven University of Technology, Netherlands
[15] Li Ren Huang, Chia Ming Tsai, Cheng Yu Chien, Chien Fu Chang, Day Uei Lee; Chip set design for 10GB/S optical transceiver; 2004 IEEE Asia-Pacific Conference on Circuits and Systems
[16] O. Kibar, D. Van Blerkom, F. Chi, and S. Esener, \Power minimization and technology comparisons for digital free-space optoelectronic interconnections," Journal of Lightwave Technology, vol. 17, pp. 546{555, Apr. 1999};
[17] C. Fan, B. Mansoorian, D. Vanblerkom, M. Hansen, V. Ozguz, S. Esener, and G. Marsden, \Digital free-space optical interconnections: a comparison of transmitter technologies," Applied Optics, vol. 34, pp. 3103{3115, June 1995}.
[18] Jim A. Tatum* and James K. Guenter Honeywell VCSEL Optical Products The VCSELs are Coming TO BE PUBLISHED IN SPIE PROCEEDINGS 4994
[19] R Kirchain, F.R. Field III,Cost Modeling of Materials and manufacturing process, Encyclopedia of Materials Science & Engineering,V2 pp 1718-27],
[20] R. Kirchain, E.Fuchs, Mapping the Cost Drivers in Optoelectronics Production, CTR
[21] Busch 1988, Ph.D. Thesis , MIT
[22] [J.P.Clark, R.Roth, F.Field , Techno-economic issues in material Selection, MIT
[22] Alcatel Ethernet-over-xDSL Complete Proposal Ethernet in the first Mile Raleigh NC, January 14-16 2002
[23] U. Gliese , M. Bruun IEEE PHOTONICS TECHNOLOGY LETTERS, VOL. 10, NO. 3, MARCH 1998
[24] Daniel Colladon, 1841Pat.# 247229; 1841
[25] [3.46 class , Prof. Kimerling, MIT 2005]

[26] Takaaki Ishigure, Hideki Endo, Kunihiro Ohdoko, and Yasuhiro Koike; High-Bandwidth Plastic Optical Fiber With W-Refractive Index Profile, IEEE PHOTONICS TECHNOLOGY LETTERS, VOL. 16, NO. 9, SEPTEMBER 2004
[27] Anilkumar Appajaiah Climatic Stability of Polymer Optical Fibers (POF) Dissertation Mathematisch-Naturwissenschaftlichen Fakultät der Universität Potsdam 16 August 2004
[28] L. Pauling and E. Wilson, Introduction to Quantum Mechanics (McGraw Hill Book Company, New York, 1935), p. 274
[29] W. Groh, Makromol. Chem. 189, 2861 – 2874 (1988)
[30] Kaino, T., Polymer Optical Fibers - Polymers for Lightwave and Integrated Optics, Editor: Hornak, L.A., Marcel Dekker, Inc., New York, ISBN 0-8247-8697-1, 1992, pp. 1-38
[31] Groh, W., Macromolecular Chemistry, 189, 1988, pp. 2861-2874
[32] Zubia, J., Arrue, J., Optical Fiber Technology. 7. 2001, pp. 101-140.;
[33] Koike, Y., Ishigure, T., IEICE Trans. Electron. E82-C, 8, 1999, pp. 1553-1559.
[34] Zubia, J., Arrue, J., Optical Fiber Technology, 7, 2001, pp. 101-140.
[35] Onishi, T., Murofushi, H., Watanabe, Y., Takano, Y., Yoshida, R., Naritomi, ,Proceedings of the Polymer Optical Fibers (POF) Conference, 1998, pp. 39-42
[36] Odian, G.,Principles of Polymerization, 3rd Edition, John Wiley and Sons, Inc.,New York, ISBN 0-47161-0208, 1991
[37] Stickler, M., Rhein, T., Polymethacrylates, Ullamann's Encyclopedia of Industrial Chemistry, Editors: Elvers, B., Hawkins, S., G. Schultz, 5th Edition, VCH Publishers, Inc., A.21, 1992
[38] W.Daum, J. Krause, P. Zamzow, O. Ziemann, " POF for data communication", 2000
[39] www.pofto.com
[40] G,D, Khue;. POF 2000
[41] www.chromisfiberoptics.com
[42] Anilkumar Appajaiah Climatic Stability of Polymer Optical Fibers (POF) Dissertation Mathematisch-Naturwissenschaftlichen Fakultät der Universität Potsdam 16 August 2004
[43] http://www.sigmaaldrich.com/img/assets/3900/Fluoromonomers_and_fluoropolymers_for_optapp.pdf
[44] Daum, W., Krauser, J., Zamzow, P.E., and Ziemann, O., POF-Polymer Optical Fibers for Data Communication, Springer-Verlag, Berlin Heidelberg, ISBN 3- 540-42009-6, 2002
[45] T. Ouchi, A. Imada, T. Sato, and H. Sakata Direct Coupling of VCSELs to Plastic Optical Fibers Using Guide Holes Patterned in a Thick Photoresist IEEE PHOTONICS TECHNOLOGY LETTERS, VOL. 14, NO. 3, MARCH 2002
[46] Information Gatekeepers (IGI)
[47]www.mostcorporation.com

[48] S.Pizzi, " Internet and T V convergence", New York, N.Y. 2001
[49] Wei-hsiu Ma and David H. C. Du; "Reducing Bandwidth Requirement for Delivering Video Over Wide Area Networks With Proxy Server", IEEE TRANSACTIONS ON MULTIMEDIA, VOL. 4, NO. 4, DECEMBER 2002 539
[50] www.ivci.com
[51] NAB T V TechCheck, National Association of Broadcasters, Washington, D.C., Feb1,1999
[52] standards.ieee.org
[53] www.mitsubishi.com
[54] www.passave.com
[55] arstechnica.com/news
[56] Information Gatekeepers Inc., "First Quarter 2005 H-S Access Report" Feb 7, 2005
[57] www.igigroup.com
[58] T. Matsuoka, T. Ito and T. Kaino, "First plastic ptical fibre transmission experiment using 520nm LEDs with intensity modulation/direct detection ELECTRONICS LETTERS 26th October 2000 Vol. 36
[59] www.ifm.liu.se/matephys/nanopto/QWires.html
[60] M.Bass, Fiber Optics Handbook
[61] I.Hayashi, M.B. Panish , and P.W.Foy, " Junctions Lasers which operate Continuously at Room Temperature", Appl.Phys.Lett. 17:109 (1970)
[62] P. Schnitzer, M. Grabherr, R. J¨ager, F
[63] R. Michalzik, P. Schnitzer, U. Fiedler, D. Wiedenmann, and K. J.Ebeling, "High-bit-rate data rate transmission with short-wavelength VCSEL's: Toward bias-free operation," IEEE J. Select. Topics Quantum Electron., vol 3, pp. 396–404, Apr. 1997
[64] K. L. Lear, V. M. Hietala, H. Q. Hou, M. Ochiai, J. J. Banas, B. E. Hammons, J. C. Zolper, and S. P. Kilcoyne, "Small and large signal modulation of 850 nm oxide-confined vertical cavity surface emitting lasers," OSA Trends in Opt. and Photon., vol. 15, pp. 69–74, 1997
[65] D. L. Huffaker, D. G. Deppe, K. Kumar, and T. J. Rogers, "Native-oxide defined ring contact for low threshold vertical-cavity lasers," Appl. Phys. Lett., vol. 65, pp. 97–99, 1994
[66] Y. Hayashi, T. Mukaihara, N. Hatori, N. Ohnoki, A. Matsutani, F.Koyama, and K. Iga, "Lasing characteristics of low-threshold oxide confinement InGaAs-GaAlAs vertical-cavity surface-emitting lasers," IEEE Photon. Lett., vol 7, pp. 1324–1326, 1995
[67] Mederer, R. Michalzik, D. Wiedenmann, and K. J. Ebeling, GaAs VCSEL's at 780 and 835 nm for Short-Distance 2.5-Gb/s Plastic Optical Fiber Data Links IEEE PHOTONICS TECHNOLOGY LETTERS, VOL. 11, NO. 7, JULY 1999 767
[68] Fibercomm. Ltd 2003
[69] Renaud Stevens, Anita Risberg", Richard Schatza, Rickard Marcks Von Wurtembergb, Bertil High-speed visible VCSEL for POF data links Kronlundb, Marco Ghisoni'' and Klaus Streubel' SPIE Vol. 3946 (2000)
[70] [Jim A. Tatum* and James K. Guenter Honeywell VCSEL Optical Products The VCSELs are Coming TO BE PUBLISHED IN SPIE PROCEEDINGS 4994
[71] Jim A. Tatum* and James K. Guenter Honeywell VCSEL Optical Products The VCSELs are Coming TO BE PUBLISHED IN SPIE PROCEEDINGS 4994
[73] K.Wada, J.F. Liu, S. Jongthammanurak, D.D.Cannon, D.T. Danielson, Y. Ishikawa, A. Eshed, C.Y.Hong, J.Michel, L.C.Kimerling; "Direct integration of Ge Detectors and modulators on the Si Microphotonics Platform"; IEEE2004, International Conference on Group IV Photonics
[74] [G. Wöhl, C. Parry, E. Kasper, M. Jutzi, M. Berroth, SiGe Pin-Photodetectors Integrated on Silicon Substrates for Optical Fiber Links ISSCC 2003 / SESSION 21 / TD: ORGANIC AND NANOSCALE TECHNOLOGIES / PAPER 21.4

[75] Lorenzo Colace, Gianlorenzo Masini, and Gaetano Assanto Ge-on-Si Approaches to the Detection of Near-Infrared Light IEEE JOURNAL OF QUANTUM ELECTRONICS, VOL. 35, NO. 12, DECEMBER 1999 1843
[76] G. Wöhl, C. Parry, E. Kasper, M. Jutzi, M. Berroth, SiGe Pin-Photodetectors Integrated on Silicon Substrates for Optical Fiber Links ISSCC 2003 / SESSION 21 / TD: ORGANIC AND NANOSCALE TECHNOLOGIES / PAPER 21.4
[77] K.Wada, J.F. Liu, S. Jongthammanurak, D.D.Cannon, D.T. Danielson, Y. Ishikawa, A. Eshed, C.Y.Hong, J.Michel, L.C.Kimerling; "Direct integration of Ge Detectors and modulators on the Si Microphotonics Platform"; IEEE2004, International Conference on Group IV Photonics
[78] Jifeng Liu, Douglas D. Cannon, -rni Wada, Samerkhae Jongthammannrak, David T. Danielson, Jurgen Michel, and Lionel C.Kimerling; Strain-engineered Ge photodetectors on Si platform for broad band. . optical communications; 2003 Optical Society of America
[79] K. Washio, "SiGe HBT and BiCOMS Technologies for Optical Transmission and Wireless Communication Systems," Central Research Laboratory, Hitachi Ltd. IEEE Transctions on Electron Devices, Vol. 50, No. 3, March 2003.
[80] Clemens J T 1997 Bell Lab. Tech. J. Autumn 76
[81] [ftp://download.intel.com/labs/eml/download/EML opportunity.pdf
[82] [CT R, MIT]
[83] Soref R A 1993 Proc. IEEE 81 1687], [Bisi O, Campisano S U, Pavesi L and Priolo F (ed) 1999 Silicon Based Microphotonics: from Basics to Applications (Amsterdam: IOS Press
[84] Masini G, Colace L and Assanto G 2002 Mater. Sci. Eng. B 89 2–9
[85] WINTERGREEN RESEARCH, INC.REPORT # SH29821338 473
[86] Pavesi L, Gaponenko S and Dal Negro L (ed) 2003 Towards the First Silicon Laser (NATO Series vol 93) (New York: Kluwer)
[87] L Pavesi Will silicon be the photonic material of the third millenium? J. Phys.: Condens. Matter 15 (2003) R1169–R1196
[88] Michael E. Groenert, Christopher W. Leitz, Arthur J. Pitera, and Vicky Yang, Harry Lee and Rajeev J. Ram, Eugene A. Fitzgerald; Monolithic integration of room-temperature cw GaAsÕAlGaAs lasers on Si substrates via relaxed graded GeSi buffer layers; JOURNAL OF APPLIED PHYSICS VOLUME 93, NUMBER 1
[89] Michel, Zheng, MIT
[90] Csutak S M, Schaub J D, Wu W E, Shimer R and Campbell J C 2002 J. Lightwave Technol. 20 1724

[91] Yang M, Rim K, Rogers D L, Schaub J D, Wleser J J, Kuchta D M, Boyd D C, Rodier F, Rabidoux P A, Marsh J T, lcknor A D, Yang Q, Upham A and Ramac S C 2002 IEEE Electron. Device. Lett. 23 395

[92] J.Liu, J.Michel, W. Giziewichz, D.Cannon, S. Jongthammanurak, D.Danielson, D.Pan, J. Yasaitis, K.Wada, L.C.Kimerling; "A 20 GHz Tensile Strained Ge photodetector on Si Platform with broad detection spectrum for optical communications and on chip applications"; 2004 IEEE

[93] Pal B P 1993 Progress in Optics vol 32, ed E Wolf (Amsterdam: Elsevier)

[94] [Miya T 2000 IEEE J. Sel. Top. Quantum Electron. 6 38

[95] Bulla D A P et al 1999 IMOC 99 Proc. IEEE p 454] [Hilleringmann U and Goser K 1995 IEEE Trans. Electron. Devices 42 84 1

[96] Cocorullo G, Della Corte F G, Iodice M, Rendina I and Sarro P M 1998 IEEE J. Sel. Top. Quantum Electron. 4 983

[97] Kimerling L C 2000 Appl. Surf. Sci. 159/160 8

[98] Jalali B, Yegnanarayanan S, Yoon T, Yoshimoto T, Rendina I and Coppinger F 1998 IEEE J. Sel. Top. Quantum Electron. 4 938]

[99] Bestwick T 1998 48th IEEE Conf. on Electronic Components and Technology (May 1998) pp 566 71

[100] Kato K and Tohmori Y 2000 IEEE J. Sel. Top. Quantum Electron. 6 4

[101] Hilleringmann U and Goser K 1995 IEEE Trans. Electron. Devices 42 841

[102] Brian E. Lemoff, Lisa A. Buckman, Andrew J. Schmit, and David W. Dolfi; "A Compact, Low-Cost WDM Transceiver for the LAN", Agilent Laboratories 2004

[103] E.Zhang, MIT M.eng thesis, 2004

[104] M.Speerchneider, MIT thesis,2004

[105]] [T. Ouchi, A. Imada, T. Sato, and H. Sakata Direct Coupling of VCSELs to Plastic Optical Fibers Using Guide Holes Patterned in a Thick Photoresist IEEE PHOTONICS TECHNOLOGY LETTERS, VOL. 14, NO. 3, MARCH 2002

[106] A.Keltic, Ph.D. Thesis ,MIT 2005

76

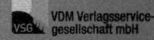

Printed by Books on Demand GmbH, Norderstedt / Germany